Whoever finds the gold of the Guadalupes must die. That was the legend. The gold was cursed. But after Old Wickiup's startling revelation, the curse was only part of the problem.

A half-white Apache boy tricks—or thinks he tricks—the old chief into revealing the place the Apaches found him as a small child. The place turns out to be the hiding place of Apache gold, a secret as closely guarded as the boy's own past.

Arizona Boy, curious about his origins and equally curious about the gold, sets out to solve the mysteries, taking with him only an old map, considerable natural cunning and common sense, and Moon Dance —a fast, loyal, beautiful Apache horse.

From the moment he rides away from Mescalero Town under "a million Apache stars," he finds himself involved in deadly games of hide-and-seek with trigger-happy El Lobo, the phantom Head Toter, gangs of outlaws and bandits, and an Apache tracking party led by Sheriff Missing Toe. When he finally reaches Dead Man's Gulch and the treasure, the situation becomes desperate and the curse of the Apache gold is about to claim another victim. But great daring, good luck, and the most fantastic ride in the history of the west bring the story to an all-revealing conclusion. With a wealth of vivid description, high humor, and a cast of entertaining characters, author Rex Benedict presents a truly exciting mystery of the old west.

This is a Junior Literary Guild selection, chosen as an outstanding book for older readers (C Group).

Good Luck Arizona Man

REX BENEDICT

Good Luck Arizona Man

PANTHEON BOOKS

Library of Congress Cataloging in Publication Data
BENEDICT, REX, *1920— Good luck Arizona man.*
SUMMARY: *A half-white Apache boy sets out to solve the mystery of his own origins and the hiding place of a treasure in gold.*
[*1. Apache Indians—Fiction. 2. Buried treasure—Fiction. 3. The West—Fiction*] *I. Title.* PZ7.B4319Go [*Fic*] *72–445*
ISBN 0–349–82441–5 ISBN 0–394–92441–X (*lib. bdg.*)

*I am still wandering
through those ghostly realms
where ancient gods
of unrelenting memory
still rise at night
to mock me
with the bitter secret
of that golden door
which ever mocked
my title of Conquistador.*

For Esteban, Cabeza de Vaca, Andres Dorantes,
Alonso del Castillo, Francisco Vásquez de Coronado,
Antonio de Espejo, Don Juan de Oñate,
and
Giusi

CONTENTS

1 · *Some Causes of Sweet Fortune* · *3*

2 · *What Old Wickiup Didn't Say* · 7

3 · *Plottin'* · *14*

4 · *On the Trail* · *22*

5 · *El Lobo Strikes* · *28*

6 · *A Tied-Up Man* · *33*

7 · *Sutler's Map* · *41*

8 · *Revelations* · *47*

9 · *The Phantom* · *53*

10 · *Headin' for Enemy Territory* · *58*

11 · *Buzzards and Dry Rivers* · *65*

12 · *A Killer Storm* · *73*

13 · *Chickens in the Coop* · *80*

14 · *More Chickens in the Coop* · *86*

15 · *I Hear Me Mentioned* · *92*

16 · *Everything Is Beautiful* · *98*

17 · *Through Dead Man's Gulch* · *106*

18 · *Night and the Phantom* · *113*

19 · *A Kind of Sadness* · *119*

20 · The Gold · 126

21 · A Mysterious Hoot Owl · 132

22 · Up to the Rim · 138

23 · Dealer's Choice · 143

24 · Under a Comanche Moon · 150

25 · Moon Dance Runs · 156

26 · Goodbye Goodbye · 163

27 · In the Aftertime · 167

Good Luck Arizona Man

1

Some Causes of Sweet Fortune

HERE ON APACHE wings of truth begins my tale. May it be worthy.

My name's Arizona Slim. 'Tain't my real name or my only name, but that don't matter. I've passed the rise and fall of many moons with the Mescaleros—them's Apaches—and I observe the tribal customs and taboos, 'specially when they're useful to me. Apaches don't like to use real names. It's bad luck. And nothin' scares an Apache like bad luck.

In fact, nothin' scares an Apache but bad luck, 'cept two or three other things what I won't mention, it bein' bad luck to do so. They got all kinds of sayin's in the tribe about bad luck, but they're hard for me to turn from the Apache language to my natural tongue, which honesty forces me to admit is a little unnatural to me but which I take proud delight in the strict and careful use of. Anyway, Apaches don't like bad luck, so they spend a lot of time, about half their lives I'd say, namin' and renamin' things—themselves mostly —just to keep their lives protected from the ravages of sorry fortune.

As I indirectly said, I was not born a pure Apache,

but of a race more fair and long of limb and, the old chiefs used to say, more cunning too. I am, however, careful with my luck. And I've always had good luck, too, which the Mescaleros say is hard for their heads to understand, considerin' my impurity. The old chiefs always used to tell me that my good luck came from the changin' of my name when I was still too young to remember. But I couldn't put my faith in that 'cause secretly I did remember. I had a memory of a name which I was sure was mine, along with two or three other memories, the main one bein' a beautiful grassy knoll what stuck like a vision in my mind. My preference in the matter is that it was the magic in my first Apache name that made my fortunes ever sweet as summer breezes on the mesa. You see, I originally possessed in the remote moontime of my pre-Apache days an American name—high or low in honor I cannot rightly say. But when a raiding party of Mescaleros under old Chief Wickiup found me, or so they always said, tribeless and alone in the rainbow land of Arizona, they took me back with them to their home in New Mexico and gave me the tribal name of Good Luck Arizona Man.

'Course I couldn't use the name, it bein' bad luck to breathe it aloud. But I kept it ever pleasant in the secret regions of my mind along with the memory of my original name, often wondering about them both and about my life before the Mescaleros found me.

Moons passed and my wonder grew. I soon learned that the Apaches keep such mysteries as darkly hidden as they try to keep the mystery of their secret gold. I wasn't as curious about the gold as I was about myself, and even as a little Apache kid I knew more about the former than the latter. Not that the Apaches can't keep a secret; it's just that they gossip all the time, and kids listen. And then there was all those tribal legends what some old chief was always recountin' and sometimes forgettin' himself in the process, if he was real old, and tellin' all the secrets. The legends would get all mixed up with the truth, and the truth would get all mixed up with the secrets and I don't know how anybody ever kept 'em straight. Even as kids we used to play games about that gold and about the Spanish conquistadors what came to get it. I was always Coronado, for the color of my hair, I think. The other kids would tell me wild tales of golden cities and lead me around in circles pointin' this way and that and hidin' their laughter behind their hands while sendin' me off across the desert in the wrong direction. And then we went to school and Miss Utter Delight, as we called our teacher, taught us more about the conquistadors and the golden cities and a lot of other things what none of us much cared about. By the time I could read and write I think I could've told you how to find the Gold of the Guadalupes, as it was called. But I couldn't 've told you a thing about myself, 'cept that I was a fair-haired Apache kid with a beautiful name I couldn't speak aloud for fear of bringin' ruin down upon myself for the rest of my natural life.

And so my curiosity grew. But a few years later

when I had got some experience in the poetical and, as the Navajos say, devious ways of Apache reasoning, I put my Apache lore and my school lore and all my natural sneakiness to work and tricked Old Wickiup into a certain secret revelation about the unsolved riddle of my beginnings.

What I found out would've devastated a normal human being, by which I mean anyone who wasn't at least part Apache. What Old Wickiup said, or more rightly what he didn't say, set my mind to soarin' high on eagles' wings and started me on a trail so wild that only an Apache could've followed it, and only a good-luck man like me could've survived to tell the tale.

2

What Old Wickiup Didn't Say

I'LL TELL YOU what Old Wickiup didn't say in just a minute. First I got to make confession, like Padre Glorio used to tell sinners at the Mission to do.

I have said I tricked the chief. I have spoken rash. Maybe I tricked him and maybe I didn't. To this day I don't know for sure and I got no wish to brag 'cause that's bad luck too. The chief had got a little infirm in the head by then and maybe he let the secret slip out unawares. You could never tell about the old ones in those days. They all seemed a little crazy in the head. He was prob'ly older than Geronimo, who was still alive at the time. And his mind was always slippin' around poetic-like somewhere in the misty times of bygone moons what nobody else in the tribe had any remembrance of unless it was his wife Mad Woman. Also he doted on me with Apache fondness, due I always thought to my impure extraction. But considerin' all that happened to me as a result of that moment, if Old Wickiup had really been fond of me he wouldn't 've let the secret out, no matter how infirm or crazy he was. So maybe it was the natural cunning of my race, as the Apaches say of Navajos and white men, what brought me the revelation. That is one of the darkest mysteries of my life and I will be ponderin' it at the moonset of my days.

Now, what Old Wickiup didn't say.

We was sittin' summer-soft one mornin' near Mescalero Town outside Old Wickiup's wickiup. And though his brush and bramble hut looked like a hundred years of bad luck, his Apache soul, I could tell, was just beginnin' to soar in summer-sweet agreement with the earth on which his bones reposed in squatted peace. He was about to relieve himself of some of the burdens of tribal knowledge for the benefit of men less old and wise, which in his case meant everybody. Already he was mumblin' low and sing-song-like about the old moontimes and the purity of ancient things and the need for the young to listen to the songs of the old.

Na-na-na.

That's what he sounded like while swayin' on his blanket and thinkin' of what to say next.

Na-na-na.

He had a good audience, kids and dogs mostly, the latter always howlin' along with any old chief who happened to be singin', 'specially on the high notes. Apache dogs like to howl. They howl all the time, 'cept when someone's dyin.' I don't know how they know. In the crowd of kids was Fantail and his brother Poop, the only two Apaches I ever knew who'd use their real names, the names bein' so impure and un-Apache that it didn't matter anyhow. Their

luck never was much good. Neither was that of Missin'
Toe, the reservation sheriff. His name wasn't pure
Apache either. He'd got it as a result of damages done
to himself with a pistol while tryin' to arrest somebody.
In back a little ways was old Mad Woman, cursin' low
and keenin' and drapin' Old Wickiup's laundry over a
greasewood bush to dry. Some of the elders of the
tribe was squatted around too, just to jog Old Wickiup's mind if it trailed off somewhere or wake him up
if he fell asleep, which sometimes happened.

Na-na-na-na. His voice was risin' higher. *Na-na-na-
na.*

Old Wickiup was a slow starter in the songs he sang,
but once he got to soarin' and the rhythm was right
and the weather was good and the people around him
was makin' sign for him to clear up somethin' by re-
peating it, he kinda lost himself in the clouds of poetry.
That was when he'd seem to get the legends and the
secrets and even the gossip all mixed up together.

Na-na-na-na.

The chant was risin' higher now and the dogs was
howlin' good.

Na-na-na-na.

His chant told of the tribe's beginnings at the ends
of the earth in northern lands where, he said, the world
had started too. Then he sloped along the mountains in
migration to the present homeland, his tale disrupted
only now and then by someone makin' sign or by the
protests of the dogs, neither of which he paid much
attention to.

Na-na-na-na.

I kept my hand ready to make sign. Anything you didn't understand you could make sign for the chief to repeat. With Old Wickiup you had to make sign at the exact right moment. If you signed too soon or too late you might just as well not signed at all. I watched him close, waitin' patiently.

And on he went, soarin' good now, 'cause he was approachin' more recent glories and the heroes of livin' memory, his memory of course. The dogs was howlin' louder too now and so was old Mad Woman. That always happened when she thought Old Wickiup was about to give away some tribal secret or another, like for instance the location of the Apache gold. I guess you couldn't much blame her for howlin' like a coyote every time the chief got careless in his tale, 'cause that gold was not only supposed to be kept a secret but sacred too. The same was true, I found out later, of my origins.

Na-na-na-na.

He was gettin' poetical now like he always did towards the end of his devotions, mixin' up names and places in wild confusion, jumpin' around a lot in time and makin' little revelations that only a quick Apache ear could catch and only then if it knew what it was listenin' for, which mine did. Still, patiently I waited.

And then my moment came. I'll always believe it was my instincts what told me. Just as he soared off through the tree tops of his memory and sailed into the rainbow land on the wings of heroic names like

Cochise and Mangas Colorados and Victorio and Nana, I signed for him to repeat. When an Apache starts chantin' about Cochise and others of livin' memory he's also chantin' about certain white people of livin' memory.

My timin' was good, couldn'ta been better. I knew how long it took him to stop. He had to go on down through Geronimo and three or four other grandfathers before the sign from my lifted hand could reach his mind and halt him in his flight. Mad Woman knew that too. Her howls rose and she looked at me with what I rightly took for murder in her eyes.

Na-na-na-na.

There was some poetical mumblin' then and then some words about the summer when the Apaches found a good-luck man.

I had him.

I signed for a repeat, for more details. With every sign I made, Mad Woman screamed. Now the rest of the tribe was gettin' nervous too, sensin' as they did that Apache games—subtle and deceitful—was bein' played.

Na-na-na-na.

Old Wickiup soared away into the deserts and mountains of Arizona, mixin' up the beauties and the names in fine disorder. He soared for a long time, namin' every rock and tree in the land where they had found the good-luck man.

I discounted everything he said and signed again. Now he was in a kind of dream-like frenzy, forgettin' himself. This was the moment when he might say anything, let slip all the secrets. Mad Woman hissed and howled and flopped her laundry over the bushes.

Na-na-na-na.

Old Wickiup flowed into tales of the Rio Grande, cursin' the Mexicans and other ancient enemies as he went. But I knew he was still on the subject of the good-luck man, and, I thought, the gold too.

I raised my hand and signed again.

He began a long lament about the strayed Apaches in Oklahoma, scoldin' them in passin' for marryin' out of the tribe.

I signed again. Mad Woman was screamin' steady now and glarin' at me with that murderous look in her eye.

Then, so quickly I almost missed it, it happened. Old Wickiup did a crazy thing, crazy even for an Apache. He swept on the wings of eagles over the length and breadth of the whole Apache world, ancient and modern, namin' each place in the old manner and not leavin' out a stream or a bush or a lizard, not leavin' out a thing, it seemed, even down to the rattlesnakes and bears and pumas, until there, finally, it was for everyone to hear by its silence—the secret. *Dead Man's Gulch.* His lips had not pronounced those words, and now his song was ended. I, Good Luck Arizona Man, had been found at Dead Man's Gulch in the Guadalupe Mountains of Texas. And that, I knew, was where the gold was too.

Things got a little hysterical then, Mad Woman

wailin' and tearin' her hair in signs of grief, the kids clappin' for joy, the dogs bayin', and Missin' Toe drawin' his gun and startin' to shoot at what I suppose he thought was danger in the air.

I made no more sign. It wouldn't 've done any good anyway. Old Wickiup had gone to sleep, sittin' straight up, sublime in his dignity.

3

Plottin'

NO APACHE EVER does anything, no matter how crazy, without a reason. Whatever Old Wickiup's reason was for makin' the revelation, I couldn't figure it out. The only thing what made sense, Apache sense, was that the chief had forgot where the gold was, lost it, and now wanted somebody to find it for him so he could die in peace. He knew how curious I was about my origins. I had asked him many times about them and he had always said, "Be patient, my son, be patient." Maybe he had mislaid that secret too. He could forget anything. If he forgot about somethin' long enough it had a way of goin' out of existence. The wonder now was that he even remembered that he had forgot.

One thing was certain. He had tied the two secrets —the place of my origins and the gold—together in a knot so tight that I couldn't think of one without thinkin' of the other. And I'm sorry to say that I always ended up thinkin' more about the gold than about my origins, no matter how I started out. I guess it had somethin' to do with my impure blood, 'cause a pure Apache don't feel the same enchantments that other people feel about gold. They like to keep it buried, knowin' as they do the grief and trouble what comes with it.

And then there was that curse which every little Apache kid knows about from the time he can crawl. *Whoever finds the gold of the Guadalupes must die.* I'd heard it all my life, and all my life I'd longed to know if it was true . . . 'cause if there's one thing I can't stand it's an unsolved mystery. I had to find out, not only about the gold but about myself as well. So I set about to plot my departure from Mescalero Town.

It pleases me to state that I did my plottin' with cold-blooded Apache guile, by which I mean I went about it like a pure blood. Apache plottin', like Apache thinkin', is poetical and devious. Everyone admires an artful plotter, even his enemies. And anyone who starts to plot always discovers that he's got enemies. I knew that Apache eyes was watchin' me, though I didn't always know whose. I could feel them in the air around the trading post and from the wickiups down the hill and sometimes from the wooden shacks along the creek.

I lived in one of the wooden shacks. Bein' a good Apache I didn't pay much attention to where I lived in those days, one place bein' about as good as another. I did pay attention to the watchin' eyes though. I like to know who my enemies are.

I think some of my White Eye nature came out in

my plottin' too. I not only dusted up my trail and laid false sign in all directions like a pure Apache, but I also put the refinements of my educated mind to work in what I'd noticed was the White Eye way of workin' out deceptions. Like most things between the two races—who never did understand each other—they're exact opposites. Apaches plot poetical; white men plot methodical. Naturally I used a little of both, likin' as I always do to have every possible advantage.

For the first time in my life—I guess I was maybe twelve, maybe thirteen at the time, and tall for my age —I had me some regrets that I hadn't studied harder at the reservation school. I began to see why White Eye kids go to school so long and study so hard. It's where they learn to plot. They use facts and figures the way an Apache uses his eyes and ears and nose. They also write things down and keep 'em straight. No White Eye chief would've ever lost a gold mine like Old Wickiup did. And if he had lost it or mislaid it or forgot about it he wouldn't 've had to put on a big show the way the chief did to try and get some-body to find it for him. He would've just looked at a book or a map or a paper of some kind and frowned the way they do and put his finger on a certain spot and maybe grunted a little, like a true chief. Then he would've gone and got it, after the necessary plottin' of course.

But I've never been one to linger long upon regret. Even as a boy I let it slip into the desert wind like withered cactus flowers, never to return.

And so, when I had misled every Indian in the tribe into thinkin' that I was goin' to Window Rock to haggle with the Navajos for a silver belt buckle what I badly needed, I turned my mind to more methodical deceits. Though I knew every rock and bush on the Mescalero reservation, and every cactus plant and grain of sand on the surrounding desert, there was a lot I didn't know about the Guadalupe Mountains. I knew it was a wild place full of wild and crazy men all lookin' for the gold and all prob'ly bein' looked for by Texas sheriffs. I'd heard stories about a madman named El Lobo what fancied the mountains and the gold belonged to him and would shoot anybody that crossed his sights. It was said that he had been there so long that he had forgotten how to talk. And there was another tale about a spook nobody had ever seen who was said to travel only at night and carry a human head around in his hands.

There was lots of stories and I believed 'em all. Most of the Apaches did, though not many of 'em had been any closer than I had to Dead Man's Gulch. Even though the Guadalupes was the ancient Mescalero homeland, no one but the old chiefs knew much about the place, the Texans bein' mean about Apaches and not permittin' them to go there even for ceremonies. 'Course that don't mean they didn't go. There's no place you can keep an Apache from goin' if he's of a mind to. I knew the old chiefs sometimes went down there, and gossip in the camp said they always brought back a few chunks of the gold, though I never knew anybody what actually seen one. But I'd never been there, and my cautious nature wouldn't let me set my foot on a piece of earth I didn't know as well as the palm of my hand. So I slipped down the hill and through the window of the reservation school.

Except for desks and books, the school was empty. I don't know if it was a regular school day or not. Apache kids don't ever seem to learn the regular days from the others. At least that's the way it used to be. We'd go when we felt like it, and we wouldn't if we didn't. I started first with the maps. I meant to take a look at the Guadalupes and at the trail of Coronado and his conquistadors. Just as I was gettin' goin' good, I sensed I wasn't alone. I couldn't tell where she came from, but suddenly there she was, standin' right behind her desk and sayin', "Arizona Boy, what an utter de-light."

No Apache ever jumps, and I didn't jump, but she did take me off my guard.

"The conquistadors," I said.

"What an utter delight," she said. "If you will just take your seat." One thing about Miss Utter Delight, she was always ready to teach—anybody, anytime, school day or not, night or day, winter or summer. All she had to do was catch you in the schoolroom. "What an utter delight." I thought she was gonna faint with pleasure. "Shall we start with Don Francisco Vásquez de Coronado, vain seeker of the seven fabled cities of Cibola?"

"Zuñi deceitments," I said.

"Deceits," she corrected.

"How come Coronado not find gold?" I asked. I was usin' my dumb voice. The dumber a kid was the more Miss Utter Delight liked him. She couldn't resist a half-wit. I put on my dumbest look and used my dumbest voice. "How come, Miss Utter Delight?" I asked.

She blinked. "Because no gold existed," she said. "Coronado's brain was doubtless affected by our desert heat."

"I think gold exist," I said.

"What an utter delight. Why did the conquistadors not find it? They searched frantically for years and years."

" 'Cause Coronado and conquistadors not know Pueblo or Apache tongue. Pueblos and Apaches make jokes. Look on map."

To my surprise she looked.

"Look for Guadalupes," I said. "How come conquistadors not look in Guadalupes for gold? Stupid maybe?"

"Not stupid," she said, lookin' at the maps.

"Crazy maybe?"

"Not crazy either." She was real busy now, not payin' much attention to me or the way I talked, even forgettin' to correct me. Somethin'—I didn't know what—had caught her fancy. She put down the map and took up a book and began to turn the pages as if she knew what she was lookin' for.

"You remember El Turco?" I asked her.

She looked up in surprise. "What an utter delight,

that you should remember El Turco. My teaching has not been in vain. What about him?"

"He knew where gold was. Look on map. El Turco wanted to take Coronado to Guadalupes. He said gold was there. El Turco was only Indian tellin' Coronado truth, and Coronado killed him."

Now she had a map in one hand and a book in the other, and I could tell by the little tremblin's she made that she was nervous. She always got that way when she was about to discover somethin' what she would call an utter delight. I think she had forgot about me. She was mumblin' to herself as she turned the pages and picked up the maps. "Do you suppose . . . do you suppose?" That was what she was sayin'. "Do you suppose . . . do you suppose?" Then she got out another book and turned a lot of pages fast, still sayin' "do you suppose" and checkin' the book with the map and blinkin' her eyes and then runnin' her long finger up and down and around in a kind of circle on the map and bringin' it to a stop and standin' there dead silent for about as long as it takes the moon to rise over the Sangre de Cristo Mountains. Then very quietly as if to herself she said, "Espejo!"

I thought she said a dirty Apache word, 'cause there's one what sounds just like it.

"Espejo!" she said again. "Antonio de Espejo. Look here." She was nervous, excited, as if she'd found some long lost secret. She pointed to the map, a small one inside a book. "There are the Guadalupes. And there's Espejo's trail . . . the dotted lines that form a circle."

"Was he a conquistador?"

"Yes," she said, "several years after the time of Coronado. He was looking for the gold too. You see, he made a large circle around the Guadalupes. Look."

I looked. And what I saw caused little ripples to run over me. Exactly in the middle of that circle by Espejo or whatever his name was was Dead Man's Gulch . . . the gold. He had come close, very close. Only one thing had kept him from findin' it: he had tried to go into Dead Man's Gulch from the wrong direction. I knew enough about those mountains to know that you don't get to Dead Man's Gulch from the west. You've got to go in from the east, the Pecos River side. Apache gold, like all Apache secrets, has to be gone after backwards.

That night, before the moon was up, I slipped shadow-soft back into the schoolroom, found the book and expertly tore out the map.

4

On the Trail

MY PLOTTIN' WAS complete. Now all I needed was a horse, and I knew the one I wanted.

He was in the pastures of Cuts Plenty Throats, a magnificent black that I had gazed at in wonder the first time I ever saw him. Never had I seen such a beautiful horse. And never had a horse taken such a natural liking to me. It was as if between us there was some mysterious secret that nobody else could share. And maybe there was, 'cause the horse himself was a mystery horse. No Apache, young or old, would talk openly about him the way they talked about other horses. They would look at him and admire him but never open their lips. There was some secret, some mystery. Every time I asked Old Wickiup about the horse, he changed the subject or pretended not to hear. What little I learned came finally from an old Navajo who used to ride all the way over from Gallup just to stand on a hill and watch him run with the herd.

One day I found the old man there alone in the pasture and I asked him, "What kind of a horse is that?"

"Nobody knows for sure," he said.

"Was he born here?"

"Yes, but I think his father was stolen from a white man." Then he went back to gazin'.

That was all I ever learned. And by the time I had found that out the horse and I had become friends in that special way I mentioned before. I named him Moon Dance. There was nothin' he wouldn't do for me. I taught him to come at my call, to search for me in hidin', to lie down, to backtrack, and even to close his eyes as if asleep. I think he would've held his breath for me if I had taken the time to teach him. He was beautiful and he was loyal. I had to have him.

So I took him, concealing him in a canyon until the night of my departure.

That night soon came.

Except for a distant coyote, Mescalero Town was moondark quiet, and that was the way I wanted it. Missin' Toe was missin' too and that was also the way I wanted it. I never did feel easy, even in the dark, with a reservation sheriff around what couldn't shoot straight. It's best to keep 'em at a distance, 'specially when you're usin' a stolen horse to carry out plots what prob'ly are unlawful. I never really knew in those days what was lawful and what wasn't. No Apache did. Not even Missin' Toe, who was sworn to uphold it.

I waited until the coyote quieted down and the dogs went to sleep, then I slipped from my shack into the night. It was summer-sweet and most of the tribe was sleepin' out beneath the stars or in the wickiups, which amounts to the same thing. So I was careful not to set my foot on anything what looked or sounded or even smelt like a body—dog or human. I had to get away without bein' detected—an Apache point of honor. To get caught slippin' away in the dead of night would've been a personal disgrace meanin' I was not only unworthy but also a nuisance, which to a sleepin' Apache is worse even than bein' a traitor.

My luck, as usual, was runnin' good. I got through the main part of the camp without disturbin' anything 'cept one small puppy what wanted to play. I picked him up and squeezed him just the right amount and when I put him down he faded like a shadow into the brush. A true Apache puppy—never disturbed a leaf.

And neither did I. I reached my horse, slipped onto him and rode into the night, dark mountains on one side of me, a desert valley on the other, and over my head a million Apache stars. I was on the trail.

By dawn's first light Moon Dance and I was slippin' into the edges of the Guadalupes. We had covered a lot of ground, most of it in the desert valleys where, but for now and then a rattlesnake, the goin' was smooth. Moon Dance didn't like the rattlers any more than I did, and I hate 'em. Also we laid false sign along the way and did some backtrackin', which an Apache does no matter where he's goin', if only to see his girl friend. For all the mystery surroundin' him, Moon Dance was in every way a pure Apache horse, by which I mean he could smell a non-Apache as far as he could smell water. Without such horses as him the

Apache race prob'ly wouldn't 've survived. Without Moon Dance I wouldn't 've made it either, as you'll see.

We had just got into the high mountains of the Guadalupes when Moon Dance flung his head straight up, the whites in his eyes shinin'. Non-Apache odors was on the wind. I could tell by the way he quivered. Apache horses don't do that when they smell Apaches. They got a special kind of quiver for every outsider— a White Eye quiver, a Mexican quiver, even a Navajo quiver. And he didn't paw the earth and skitter around either. He knew how far an enemy ear to the ground can hear a horse's tramplin'. I had taught him.

I pulled in under a ledge, got off, and slipped up to the rocks above. Moon Dance would still be there when I got back, and if I didn't get back he'd go lookin' for me. There's nothin'—absolutely nothin'—like a loyal Apache horse.

Cautiously I peered out. Just below me was a man. He was big, dirty, ugly, and talkin' to himself, a real wild man. And suddenly, rememberin' the stories, I recognized him.

It was El Lobo!

He was the one with the crazy idea that the Guadalupes belonged to him. One time long ago, accordin' to the gossip, he had actually found the Apache gold. And then somethin'—Apache tricks prob'ly—happened. When he went back later to get the gold, he couldn't find the place again. The more he looked for it the crazier he got, they said. By this time I guess he was as crazy as you can get and still live. They also said he'd shoot you on sight, but bein' wild and mad and nervous-like his aim wasn't very good.

His appetite looked good. Crazy men, I've always noticed, like to eat. The crazier they are the more they like to eat. Padre Glorio used to eat all the time, and got a little crazier every day of his life. Old Wickiup on the other hand, who everybody said was crazy, ate only a nut for breakfast and a wild plum or two for supper, so I guess his craziness was of another kind. Right now El Lobo was gorgin' himself. Looked like he was eatin' a javelina, which is a wild pig the White Eyes like but an Apache won't touch. While he was eatin' he was also scratchin' himself and wipin' his mouth and kickin' rocks around as if cursin' 'em for being' rocks and not the gold he had one time held in his hands.

He wasn't a pretty sight to see, and watchin' crazy men ain't never been a favorite sport of mine, 'specially crazy outsiders. The trouble with a crazy outsider, White Eye or Mexican it don't matter, is that he don't do crazy things all the time. Crazy Apaches are always crazy. You can count on 'em and put your faith in 'em. I wouldn'ta trusted El Lobo any farther than I would a rattlesnake. His craziness wasn't the kind I was used to. I decided to slip away without disturbin' him at his meal. For some reason I didn't like bein' on the same earth with El Lobo, at least not until I got to know him better. But I knew I'd have to keep track of him and prob'ly a few others like him. Young though I was, I knew from the tales that wherever there's gold there's always somebody lookin' for it, usually a White Eye or a Mexican and usually crazy in the head. Been that way since the time of the conquistadors.

I turned away from El Lobo then and started back to my horse, takin' no particular precautions. And that was where I made my first mistake.

5

El Lobo Strikes

I DISLIKE ADMITTIN' to mistakes. It damages your reputation and, at least in my case, your pride. Most Apaches don't care if they make a mistake. All they care about is comin' out alive. The way they figure it is, if you come out alive you didn't make a mistake.

But I got to admit it. I made a mistake. I did what no Apache or anybody else ought to do—turned my back on El Lobo.

Repentance, as Padre Glorio used to say to sinners, was swift in comin'. And again it was Moon Dance who warned me. If El Lobo's odor hadn't got too overpowerin' for an Apache horse to stand, Moon Dance wouldn't 've whinnied, and if Moon Dance hadn't whinnied, this tale would never have been told.

As it was, it was close.

I heard the whinny and jumped sideways. El Lobo crashed down like a big bear right where I'd been, a huntin' knife in his hand. He hit the ground hard, cursin' loud, and rolled down the slope against a scrub tree where he laid lookin' at me kind of astonished-like and growlin'. He was old and he was filthy and he looked mean. It was the first time in my life I'd come face to face with a crazy outsider. He had no gun, that I could see. Only the knife in his hand. He was wavin' it and growlin' and grinnin' like a real idiot and slobberin' a little too and goin' "Hee hee hee" in between a jumble of words what sounded like "biondo diablo gringo muchacho muchacha." That's what it sounded like, the part I could make out. He started to get up then, still grinnin' that red-mouthed grin and hee-heein' and slobberin' and cursin' and drippin' tobacco juice from the sides of his mouth, or maybe it was froth of the kind madmen are supposed to make.

I drew my bowstring back, the arrow in it. I had no choice. It was him or me. I could feel it.

A look of puzzlement, almost of pain, crossed his crazy face. I felt kind of sorry for him, standin' there like a pitiful old bear chokin' on tobacco juice and spittle and maybe bewilderment too. But he kept makin' the "hee hee" between the drippin's. And finally he said, "Apach'?"

"Vamoose."

He started towards me then, that crazy grin still on his face. Now he was suckin' in his breath and goin' "hee hee hee" and sayin' "Gringo, Gringo, Gringo, these mountains is mine."

"Stop right there," I said.

I guess it was somethin' in my voice what did it, 'cause he stopped. But then he did another crazy thing, kind of exploded. He jumped up in the air and let loose what I would call a storm of abuse, callin' me every Mexican, White Eye and Apache name he could think of, all of 'em bad, and finishin' off with a kind of insane scream what sounded like, "These mountains is mine! These mountains is mine. These is my mountains."

I didn't think he was ever gonna stop, but when he did, I said, "Vamoose." Then I whistled low. Moon Dance came trottin' up, nosin' my backside with horsely affection. That seemed to increase his puzzlement. I guess he'd never seen an Apache what looked like me. But he had seen Apache bows and arrows. I could tell by the way he was cringin' just from lookin' at mine. I don't think he cared who or what I was, a boy or a girl or a Mexican or an Apache. It was the arrow what made him sweet and respectful. An Apache arrow does look fearsome when you're pointin' it at somebody close up, even if that somebody's a madman. I was stretchin' the string a little, and if you got an enemy and you're stretchin' the string and the arrow is pointin' at his person, he always gets furious and sweet and respectful and scared too. I could see El Lobo's fear and fury in his crazy eyes. I also saw that he had an old scar runnin' just under the brim of his hat.

"Get goin'," I said.

"My sack."

He had dropped a white sack, the kind they used to sell Bull Durham tobacco in at the tradin' post in Mescalero Town. It was the large size.

"Get goin'."

"My sack."

It hurt to look at him. It hurt to hear his voice. It

prob'ly wouldn't 've hurt a pure Apache, but it hurt me. He wanted that sack so bad. His bleary red eyes was sick with wantin'. I've seen dyin' men with eyes less wantful.

"My sack."

"Get goin', and leave the sack."

For a moment it seemed that he might risk his life, might lunge against the arrow for his sack. But when I drew the string a notch tighter he made some ugly growls and wiped the spittle from his mouth with the back of his hand and turned down the mountain. It took him about the range of an arrow before he set up the cursin' and hee-heein' again. I knew what he was sayin', threats for the most part, though I couldn't understand a word.

It didn't matter anyway, 'cause by then I'd opened the sack and saw the cause of his wild rage. The sack was full of nuggets, pure gold. I bit one and it was not much harder than a raw potato. Guadalupe gold. Apache gold. No other gold anywhere was that soft. The stories were true, then: that crazy old bear really had found it and lost it. Or maybe that scar he had beside his ear had helped him to forget where the gold was hidden. The scar had all the appearance of havin' been done by an Apache hand. I recognized the work.

A few moments later I slipped around the mountain and looked down on El Lobo below. He was still cursin', out of his mind with rage. Before he could even look up, I dropped the sack along the trail in front of him. I was almost back to Moon Dance when I heard him roar. But now it wasn't such a pitiful roar and I imagined his eyes had lost that bothersome longin'.

Moon Dance and I rode away then, victorious I guess, alive for sure. I knew I'd prob'ly meet El Lobo again and he'd prob'ly try to kill me again, 'cept next time I wouldn't turn my back—if, that is, I had a choice.

6

A Tied-Up Man

CRAZY PEOPLE NEVER bring good luck. And sure
enough, three sunsets later I ran into more trouble.

They was bad men too, but bad in a different way
than El Lobo. Some bad men you like and some bad
men you don't, just like you like some good men and
some you don't. I don't know why. Still, it's a good
thing I'm a good-luck man when it comes to dealin'
with bad men, 'cause if I wasn't I wouldn't 've found
out what I did about myself and about the gold and
some other things as well.

Moon Dance and me was deep into the Guadalupes
by then, makin' our way along the eastern slopes on
the Pecos River side where there's not much water and
lots of old bones from dead cattle what couldn't make
it to the next water hole. I had studied my stolen map,
which I carried in my leggin's along with other valu-
ables, and was followin' what I believed to be Espejo's
trail in the lost moontimes. My plan was to follow that
trail in a circle of the mountains, slow and easy like,
locatin' all the varmints, so to speak, and then go into
Dead Man's Gulch from the east.

You never really know when trouble's gonna come,

'specially when you're lookin' for gold. Mine always seemed to come not only when I least expected it but when I least wanted it. Take for instance the trouble I ran into here. Moon Dance had sniffed out a natural spring and we had made camp under the first stars. I had eat a little jerky I had in my leggin's and Moon Dance was grazin' on the dry grass. Night was comin' on and I was thinkin' about the gold and all the people I'd ever known what had anything to do with it. I was recallin' Pueblo stories and Apache stories, tryin' to remember some little hint or another what would help me. But most especially I was rememberin' somethin' I'd forgotten about what happened when I was very small.

There was an old woman. She'd come to see Old Wickiup, 'cause they was relatives or somethin'. She had moaned and tore her hair and tried to get the chief to tell her where the gold was. She said her man needed it bad. It was for the good of the Mimbreños, I think she said, and would be good for the Mescaleros too. But Old Wickiup had just wandered off the subject like he always did in serious matters and never wandered back. Finally she left and I never saw her again. She was Geronimo's wife, whose name I never knew.

It was in that moment, sittin' there beneath the stars, summer-sweet and happy as my horse, neither wantin' or needin' trouble, that I saw the smoke against the sky about two arrow flights away.

I drew back into the tall mesquite and put my ear to the ground.

As near as I could judge there was two men and three horses. The number of horses was easy to tell, they stompin' off the gnats and flies. But the men wasn't movin' around so much. That extra horse might've been a pack animal, though I knew most people movin' through those parts didn't bring along no extra burdens. In too big a hurry.

I was Apache patient, waitin' for all the stars to come out. Also I closed my eyes and opened them slow several times as I'd been taught until I could see as well in the dark as I could by day. I laid Moon Dance down flat on the sandy earth, takin' care to keep him off the bull-tongue cactus. He'd stay there without movin' until I got back or whistled or a rattler got too close. Even the most obedient Apache horse will bolt when rattlers are around, and I can't say I blame him.

A few moments later I was in close to the camp on the downwind side, concealed by rocks and sagebrush. I didn't fear about bein' seen or heard, 'cause I could see through their dirt and whiskers that they was white. But I didn't trust the horses. Apaches give off just as funny a smell to a non-Apache horse as El Lobo gave off to Moon Dance, though prob'ly not so strong. El Lobo's odor would've spooked a dead mule.

I laid still for a while, givin' the bugs and night things time to make acquaintance with my person. If I'd been spyin' on Apaches that close up they'da known by now just from the movement of little crawlin' things where I was. But these wasn't Apaches.

They was white and they was mean, carryin' guns. And I could see they was frettin' themselves about somethin'.

Then I saw what that somethin' was. Off in the shadows was another white man, tied up with a lariat.

The two ugly ones was talkin' low while they set by the fire, dippin' somethin' from a can what looked like beans, and drinkin' coffee from dirty tin cups. They was talkin' about what to do with the tied-up man. One of the men called the other Grizzly and he called him Cicero, though later I noticed they shortened their names to what sounded like Griz 'n' Cis.

Griz was strainin' coffee through his beard and noddin' towards Tied Up, which name I gave him to change his luck, and sayin' in a low voice, "One thing's fer sartin. If we kill him he cain't tell us nothin'."

"Yer right, Griz. But he ain't tellin' us nothin' nohow. I tell ya, he don't scare."

"I ain't so shore, Cis. Ol' Griz 'n' Cis'll scare him yit. I ain't never seed a man ya cain't scare."

"We done tried that, Griz. He don't scare. I ain't never seed a man so cool."

They didn't want Tied Up to hear. And they seemed in about as much bafflement as El Lobo about what to do, though they wasn't as far gone along the crazy trail.

"Maybe he really don't know," Cis said. "Maybe that's why he don't scare and he don't talk."

"He orghter scare, at least. Besides, I think he knows. Why else would he be in these mountains?

Maybe fer his health? He don't look unhealthy to me. Kinda skinny's all. If he's on the way to somewhere he'd take a stage coach, and carry some kind of papers with him to prove who he is in case he gits robbed or held up or killed or somethin'. He ain't got nothin' on him 'cept this one measly piece of paper that don't do us no good since neither of us ever knowed how to read and never will. Nope, Cis, take it from ol' Griz, he's out here a lookin' fer that gold—same as you 'n' me and the crazy Mexican and the crazy man with the Winchester that took a shot at us and the same as that demon of a beast runnin' around with that human head in his hands and gruntin' like a wild pig."

"You ain't shore it's a human head," Cis said. "We ain't ever come that close to him."

"It's a head and it's human, take it from ol' Griz. I ain't had much schoolin', Cis, but I know a human head when I see one. There was a demon like that over in the Superstitious Mountains in Arizony. One time I seen him close enough up to know that it waren't a mule's head or a coyote's head he was luggin' around. It was a real life-size human head with blood 'n' hair still on it, the last one he'd cut off. They say he hacked 'em off with a dull axe. I wonder whose head this one's luggin' around."

"Maybe we been out here too long, Griz. It's gittin' ya. Apache mountains is allers spooky. They gives ya the creeps. Ya feel like somebody's watchin' ya, and somebody prob'ly is. I got a feelin' somebody's watchin' us right now." Here Cis looked around him at the horses and the tied-up man and even at me, but if he saw anything he didn't show no sign. "And if ya git to feelin' that way and ya think about it too long somethin' happens to yer mind, even a good mind like yers, Griz. Look what happened to El Lobo. They say he once had as good a mind as you 'n' me. The Apaches musta scared him good."

"Apaches don't scare me, and El Lobo don't scare me, and the murderin' varmint with the Winchester don't scare me too much, though he ain't exactly mother's milk. But that spook luggin' that head around scares me somethin' powerful. I git the jeebies just thinkin' about him."

I could tell that it wouldn't be long before they was as crazy as El Lobo. Gold does that to you if you look for it long enough and think about it too much and don't find it. Cis was right about that.

I wondered who the third person was. He was layin' quiet, workin' at his ropes a little but not doin' much good.

"S'pose he really don't know nothin' about the gold," Cis said, noddin' towards Tied Up. You could tell from the tone of their voices that they wasn't gonna kill him. They just couldn't figure out the best way to admit it to each other. They was bad but not all bad.

"We'll try him in the mornin'," Griz said. "Check his ropes. I'll stake out the horses."

Cis went over and examined the knots with the toe of his boot. Then he came back and set down against a

saddle and pulled his dirty hat down over his eyes.
When Griz came back from stakin' out the horses he
did the same thing. They left the fire goin' and both of
'em slept with their hands clasped over their hearts,
their guns restin' on their chests. Except for the guns
they looked like they was prayin', which maybe they
was . . . for gold. In about a twinkle of a star they was
both snorin' heavy, as dead in sleep as honest men.

I don't think Tied Up even knew I was near him
until I laid my hand over his mouth, makin' signs for
him not to move. But that wasn't necessary, 'cause he
didn't even blink an eye. He was a cool one, as Cis had
said—the most casual tied-up man I believe I ever un-
tied. From the easy way he looked at me while I cut
him loose, you'd 've thought he was not only expectin'
me but that maybe he knew me too . . . smilin' friendly,
no signs of irritation, and clean, considerin' the dirt
he'd been layin' in. His hat, which was a white one,
and his tie, which was a black one, was perfectly in
place. I noticed he was lookin' at me about as close as I
was lookin' at him, though I couldn't think of anything
about myself what he could marvel at, unless it was my
Apache leggin's. I wasn't wearin' my headband, it
bein' bad for the vision. I admit my hair was pretty
long, but I still think it was too dark for him to tell just
by that that I was an Apache. Maybe it was the knife
I used to cut him loose with—a pure Apache knife.

Griz 'n' Cis went on snorin' while I brought Tied
Up's horse. I had already got him ready, which had
taken up more time than gettin' the man ready, the

horse not likin' my smell and bein' skitterish. It took me a while to quiet him down enough to get him by the nostrils and hold him Comanche style until my scent was as pretty to him as clover in the valley. Slow and careful I brought the horse up and helped Tied Up on. Then I did a crazy thing, at least crazy for an impure Apache. For a pure Apache it wouldn't 've been crazy at all, just normal Apache fun, which actually I've always thought was a little crazy most of the time. I went over to Griz 'n' Cis and gently eased their guns off their chests and out of their clasped hands. Still the snorin' did not pause. Without the guns they looked like innocents at prayer.

"Ride away slow," I said to Tied Up. They were the first words spoken.

"What about you?"

Even his voice was pleasant.

"Don't worry about me," I said. "This is my homeland."

Before he could ask any more questions I handed him the two guns, and while he was tryin' to figure out what to do with them I slipped moonlight-soft into the shadows.

He followed my advice and rode away slow.

7

Sutler's Map

MUCH AS I wanted to, I had no time that night to do any ponderin' over what I'd heard from Griz 'n' Cis, 'cause when I got back to Moon Dance I saw right off that I'd had visitors. They hadn't disturbed anything, least of all Moon Dance, which meant that they'd been Apaches. No other odor could've come that close to an Apache horse without him lettin' me know. Instead, he was still there where I'd left him, sleepin' a little. And when I let him up he whinnied low and nuzzled my backside with his nose.

It was the horse hairs from Moon Dance's tail what let me know about the visitors. Before goin' down the slope to spy on Griz 'n' Cis, I had strung a horsehair net around my camping place. A rattlesnake couldn't 've got through it without me knowin' it. When I got back and saw that the hairs had been disturbed, and not by any snake either, I knew for sure that Old Wickiup had put men on my trail and that they had found me. It didn't really surprise me and somehow it didn't bother me too much right then, though I had a feelin' it would when I found the gold.

Whoever finds the gold of the Guadalupes must die.

What kind of Apache games was Old Wickiup playin'?

But I didn't have time to give that any thought either, 'cause the mornin' colors was turnin' on the mountains now and in a little while Griz 'n' Cis would be stirrin'. I took Moon Dance a little farther down wind, 'cause the breezes of mornin' are tricky. Then I waited in concealment for the two ugly innocents to wake from prayerful dreams of gold.

Griz woke first. When he pawed around lookin' for his gun and didn't find it he kicked Cis awake and that one started pawin' too. They pawed on one side and then on the other and then rolled over and pawed underneath. When they saw the lariat and Tied Up not tied up any more, not even there, they began to wake up faster. Griz was in a state of complete bewilderment. He was sittin' on his saddle sideways holdin' his hat in his hand and mumblin' somethin' too low for me to hear. He looked just like Padre Glorio doin' what I think he called penitence.

Cis stood lookin' into the distance in all directions, like maybe the mountains was not only filled with phantoms carryin' human heads around but also phantoms what sneaked into your camp and turned prisoners loose in the middle of the night and stole your gun to boot. Then he walked slowly over to where Griz was and set down sideways on his saddle too, his hat in his hand.

They set there for a while watchin' the sun come up and shoutin' abuse at each other. Finally Griz got up and roared out what seemed to be a special curse of some kind. He wadded up a piece of paper and threw it down on the ground and stomped on it with first one foot and then the other and then kicked it until it flew into the air a little ways and hooked on a sagebrush and hung there. Then he threw his hat down hard on the ground and stomped on it for a while. And Cis just set there watchin' him and listenin' while he roared at the mountains and cursed the day that he was born and the day Tied Up was born and the day Cis was born and the day the Apaches was born and the Mexicans and the Texans and just about everybody else he'd ever knew or heard of, finally callin' down an extra special curse on a world what would let him grow to manhood without permittin' him to learn to read.

I guessed he was referrin' to the piece of paper they had taken from Tied Up, the one he had been stompin' on. It had blown farther down the slope now and when Griz got through callin' down curses on the world and everybody in it and went out to pick up the paper and saw that it had blown away he kicked at a bull-tongue cactus and started cursin' all over again—which he was still doin' when they finally saddled up and rode away into the mountains a little later.

I quickly took possession of the paper.

Back with Moon Dance, who snorted me a greeting, I took stock of my new situation. It was midmornin' now, the sun beginnin' to burn a little, and that ain't the best kind of sun to have if you ain't slept the night before. That kind of sun makes you lazy and puts you to sleep, which I couldn't let happen. Now I not only had to keep alert for Griz 'n' Cis and maybe Tied Up too but also for somebody with a Winchester rifle what liked to shoot at you, not to mention the phantom with the head and the Apaches trackin' me. Things was gittin' a mite crowded in the Guadalupes where, no matter how far you looked in any direction, you couldn't see a livin' soul. I wanted to take a look at that piece of paper but there just wasn't time. I had too many people too close to me for comfort. I was still followin' what I believed to be Espejo's trail in the lost moontimes, but bein' as I am the kind what likes to know where everybody is and what they're doin' I eased Moon Dance off the trail and down the slopes until I picked up Tied Up's tracks.

Two hours later I saw him in the distance. He was standin' on a mound, calm and cool and clean, not even tryin' to keep out of sight, lookin' through what the White Eyes calls a telescope and what the Apaches calls a long eye or sometimes Crook's eye, after our best-loved enemy what used to use one.

Tied Up looked through the telescope for a while and then went over where his horse was standin' by some big boulders. He leaned down and pulled out a kind of satchel from under one of them, folded up the telescope, put it inside, and returned the satchel to its hidin' place. Then he rode away in the direction of Guadalupe Peak, takin' no precautions of any kind, not even attemptin' any. I think it was then that I began to worry about him.

What I did next I couldn't resist doin'. And I think I oughta say that I don't share the pure Apache's love for snoopin' in other people's things. I am, for all my Indian ways, a believer in privacy. But as you know, I'm also very curious, and I just couldn't resist the temptation to look inside that satchel.

I didn't regret it, 'specially when I saw it contained a small sack of gold nuggets and under the sack a map. I tested a nugget with my teeth. Soft. Apache gold. Just like the kind El Lobo had. Then I unfolded the map. It was a map of the Guadalupe Mountains and it looked deservin' of close inspection. Just by glancin' at it I could see the Pecos River and Guadalupe Peak and Dead Man's Gulch and back of Dead Man's Gulch the high cliffs of Suicide Leap. Down at the bottom of the map some big rude hand had scrawled—SUTLERS MAP DONE BY HIM   DRAWED FROM A MAP BY JB THAT HE LENT ME AND I RETURNED   HE WAS A GOOD MAN.

I was just settlin' in against the rocks to study the map a little when I heard gunfire, lots of it, in the distance. You could tell by the stingin' sounds that it was comin' mostly from a rifle. I stuffed the map in my leggin' and laid my head to the ground, cuppin' my ear. The shootin' was still goin' on at what sounded like a murderous rate and not far up the trail I could hear Tied Up's horse goin' slowly across the terrain. Tied Up, as usual, didn't seem to be in any hurry. I knew by now that he just wasn't the kind to get excited by a little shootin'. But I was. I decided then and there to hide the satchel. So I found a small piece of chalklike rock and scratched out a message to Tied Up on the boulder under which he had hid his belongin's. I didn't worry about my Apache trackers findin' the message, 'cause if there's one thing a good Apache tracker can't do good it's read the American language. Somehow the two just don't go together. Griz 'n' Cis couldn't read either, so I didn't have to worry about them. Neither could El Lobo, if he happened to come along. All in all I guess Tied Up and me was the only two educated people in that part of the world.

My message said. YER SACHEL REHID IN GOFER HOLE 40 PASES WEST NEAR RATLSNAIK NEST. As you will note, I used deception in the spellin' . . . coverin' my tracks, so to speak.

8

Revelations

I KEPT TO the cliffs and gorges while makin' my run to the battleground. I wanted to see but not be seen, which is always the wisest way to approach a gun fight. Along the way, far in the distance now, I saw Tied Up. He was standin' atop a rock lookin' like a statue with a white hat on and makin' what appeared to be an observance of the whole world. I eased Moon Dance down into a gorge and the white hat disappeared.

It didn't take me long to find the battle, which turned out to be just half a battle, Griz 'n' Cis not havin' any guns and bein' holed up under a ledge where it looked like they'd been takin' an afternoon snooze in the shade. Up high on the rocks above them was the fellow with the Winchester, pumpin' shots down on the rocks below. Griz 'n' Cis was safe enough. Winchester couldn'ta hit 'em in a hundred moons where they was. Knowin' this, they didn't seem much worried. Griz, who I think had been sleepin' on his saddle, did get up and crawl out a little ways and look up, but then he crawled back and flopped down on the saddle again and pulled his hat down over his eyes and prob'ly called a few curses down on Winchester not so much for shootin' at him but for botherin' his sleep. Cis didn't even look up. I figured he was snorin' heavily away . . . deep in dreams of gold.

Winchester looked like a wild one, all right. He would've looked wild enough even without the gun. Like all the other mountain crazies he was filthy, his clothes in tatters and lookin' like somethin' what a pig wouldn't 've slept in, or even gone close to for that matter. His beard looked like the underneath side of a black sheep's belly, bein' a mat not only of dirt and burrs but prob'ly lice too. To an Apache that was revoltin' enough, but even more revoltin' was the cackle he made every time he fired the gun. He would jump up and down and cackle like a big crazy chicken. Then he'd crouch down and fire another shot. Then he'd cackle again. Sure seemed happy at his work.

He was still shootin' and cacklin' when I slipped away. I could hear the stings of the rifle echo up and down the mountains for a long time. I figured my trackers, bein' Apaches and not only curious but snoopy too, would stay around a while to watch the show. Crazy white men always catch their fancy. That would give me time to put some distance between them and me before night came, and since Apache trackers don't like to track at night I figured I was safe enough for the time bein'. But sooner or later, before goin' in after the gold, I had to lose them for good.

I got back on the old Espejo trail then and rode hard,

feelin' good, thinkin' of the night to come when I could study the map and the piece of paper in my leggin's and maybe also get some sleep. As usual, Moon Dance sensed my feelin's. That was, without a doubt, the finest horse what ever lived. The whole happiness of his life was to carry me on his back. I think somehow he even knew that we was goin' after gold what was secret and forbidden. He sniffed it out of my mind some way, the way ordinary horses sniff out your intentions when you head for home. But most and best of all, Moon Dance could sniff danger long before I knew it was close. If I was asleep he'd wake me. If I was at a distance he'd whinny. If we was in hidin' he'd stay quiet as long as I commanded. I actually think that if I'd got killed that horse would've somehow carried me back to Mescalero Town for a proper funeral.

Towards evenin' we found a natural spring with a little green grass around it and made camp. I ate some more of my jerky and dug up a few roots. Then I got out my maps and the paper I'd taken from Griz 'n' Cis and set to work. First I made a close inspection of Sutler's map. And it's a good thing I did, 'cause if I'd read Griz 'n' Cis's paper first I'da been in too much confusion even to see the map.

In the center of Sutler's map was a big x that marked the gold. The x was just above Dead Man's Gulch. A little farther up was Suicide Leap, a place where two mesas high in the mountains almost come together but not quite. Checkin' my other map, the one I'd taken from Miss Utter Delight's book, I saw that Espejo had tried to go into Dead Man's Gulch from the direction of Suicide Leap. Right at the moment I was sittin' south and west of Suicide Leap. Far in the distance, almost straight north, I could see the top of Guadalupe Peak, the highest point in the mountains. I took up Sutler's map again and saw that the trail to Dead Man's Gulch started at the Pecos River at a place called Horsehead Crossin'. When the trail got into the mountains there was a place marked BLUE MOUND. That was just about where I'd found Tied Up with the telescope, so I guessed he was followin' the map, which he had prob'ly set to memory. The dotted line then made a lot of windin' turns as it moved on generally westward. About halfway to the x mark was the words GO ON FOOT OR BY MULE. After that the trail led almost straight west until it came to Dead Man's Gulch with the x above it. Underneath was written, GOLD HERE 50 FEET DOWN WATCH FER RATTLERS AND APACHES.

I didn't know who Sutler was and I didn't know who JB was, but by the time I'd finished my inspection of that map I knew that somebody in the map-makin' business had been an Apache Indian. Nobody but an Apache could've marked that trail. Accordin' to my calculations, it was exact. There was only one trouble. Accordin' to Mescalero gossip you could be standin' right on top of the place what said 50 FEET DOWN and not even know it was the place. Actually there was two troubles. *Whoever finds the gold of the Guadalupes must die.* That was the other one.

I put the maps back in my leggin's then and took out the piece of paper Griz 'n' Cis had took from Tied Up and couldn't read. And for reasons that I can't clearly explain I'm thankful that them two ugly outlaws couldn't read what was on that paper. That they had pawed over it and kicked it around and mistreated it was enough to offend me in my soul. 'Cause that little piece of paper, hooked from off the wind so to speak, turned out to be a kind of sacred thing for me.

All the mysteries of my life suddenly came floating back before my eyes, things I had carried in my head for as long as I could remember. They were my first memories, things clung to, forgotten, remembered and forgotten again. One of them was the memory— blurred but real—of people whose faces I couldn't re- call callin' me William, and I always thought they called the man I was with Mr. Brodie. But I could never be sure if it was real or my imagination. Nor did the Apache habit of changin' your name every new moon help either. After a few moons of that all the names take on a kind of blur. And so the mysterious names in my mind grew dimmer and dimmer.

Then I opened that paper.

Here it is, exactly as it was put down by the same hand what scrawled the map, 'cept now for some reason his spellin' was truly sufferin' to behold and the scrawl seemed weaker. I soon saw why.

Odessy Texas
1897

The messige of a dyin' man rit by him JOHN SUTLER
to his no good son of the same name.
Dear John
This is my last recwest & testymint which I hope you
heed so my bones will RIP. By the time you git it I will
be 6 ft b'low ground here in Odessy probly which is
all rite by me cuz I dont see as how it makes any difrence
where they put you so long as they do it desently. I
send this c/o mr Connel at bank in Midland. He is a
good Texian & will tern over to you the bal. of my
acct & sack of nugets. I kno yer ma dide of over work
& yer sisters terned out pore & I warent much of a pro-
vyder but I ment well. You see son it was that gold.
It tuk me longer than I rekoned. But I aint lamintin.
On the hole I bin lucky. I did whut no man afor me
did. I fownd the gold & got owt with my hide. Others
has fownd it but didnt git owt. A Mex fownd it in '83
& some other peeple to. John Brodie fownd it in '86, I
think, cuz neether him or his little boy Willyum was
ever herd of agin & one of his horses come back to the
livry stable in Pecos with the Apache mark on it. That
was the year of the grate uprisin'. I hope you find it. It
aint easy even with Brodie map. You kin stand rite on
it & not see it. & I hope you change yer idel ways. The
life you leed aint a fittin one fer the son of a man whos
pappy fit the war fer indypendence at the alamo.

Hopin you repint, I am
yer dyin dad
John Sutler

p s   watch out fer Apaches

William Brodie. That was me.

9

The Phantom

NO APACHE, PURE or impure, ever shows surprise. At
least he's not supposed to, 'cause he's been taught not
to. Findin' out who I was was not just a surprise, it was
a revelation. But I can state with truth and pride and
without fear of braggin' that I looked right at my real
name, recognized it, and never lost one bit of my
Apache calm. Old Wickiup himself couldn't 've concealed his emotions any better.

I must admit that a lot of different thoughts was
turnin' around in what I like to call the breeze-soft
regions of my mind, which is where I keep the secrets
of myself. There was the horse—one of the horses—
blood-smeared with the Apache sign returnin' to the
livery stable. There was that map, my father's map,
which for sure an Apache hand or at least an Apache
mind had drawn. And then there was the leader of that
Apache party that had found me—Old Wickiup.
There was, as you can see, still lots of mysteries in my
mind and I knew I'd have to unravel them just as I'd
have to unravel the mystery of the gold.

The stars, beautiful and clean, was just beginnin' to
come out and I was puttin' the paper back in my leg-

gin' when Moon Dance shied towards me and then away, spookin' in a way I'd never seen him spook before. It wasn't a rattler spook or any other kind of spook I knew. It was more like he had sniffed out some new kind of earthly creature. Bein' an Apache horse, he calmed down when I told him to, but underneath his calm was a quiverin' of a kind you almost never find in a horse—fear, real fear, a kind of terror. Whatever was out there in the dark was completely strange to Moon Dance's nose. It was too dark now to see far, but whatever was lurkin' in the shadows wasn't very far away. I kept Moon Dance's nose buried in my arm so he wouldn't forget himself and bolt. So long as my odor was strong and close enough, he'd stay with me. Never heard of an Apache horse desertin'.

But I guess there's some things even the loyalest horse can't stand. Or maybe Moon Dance figured that if I didn't have sense enough to save myself he'd do it for me, 'cause he bolted, with me hangin' to the mane and boundin' on as he ran. And just as I came up on him I saw the reason for his fear. There in the shadows stood the phantom.

I felt a little shiver of my own at the sight. He looked gray in the night, a big formless blur. He was lookin' right at me and holdin' somethin' in his hands as if offerin' it to me. It was about the size of a small human head. That was all I saw, 'cause by then Moon Dance was gone, me still hangin' on.

Horses, when they really spook, don't joke. They go crazy. It takes a lot of time and patience to calm them down, 'specially if you're ridin' 'em without a bridle like I was. I never could bring myself to put a bridle on a horse or a bit in his mouth. It's degradin' for the horse. When finally I got Moon Dance calmed down a little I turned him back around in the direction of Head Toter, as I'd decided was a proper name for the phantom. But Moon Dance's quiverin' started up again as violent as before. He was doin' a kind of nervous dance, his powerful head and gleamin' eyes wild with movement and mistrust. Never saw a horse take such a dislikin' to a human, which I guessed Head Toter was. Whatever he was, I had to find out. So I put Moon Dance in hidin', careful to wind the horsehair threads around the place to let me know about visitors. Then I slipped back along the trail into the night.

A big moon was risin' now and what the White Eyes calls the Milky Way was blazin' over my head, makin' a kind of grayness on the mountains. It was for sure a spooky place, so quiet that when you breathed you sounded like a horse what had just run a race. Now and then a mountain owl hooted and I couldn't keep from wonderin' if them was my Apache trackers sendin' signals or if they was real owls. Sometimes you can't tell the difference. I slipped as soft as moonlight through the shadows, layin' my ear to the ground every few feet and sniffin' like a coyote and listenin' for disturbances of night-crawlin' things. I wasn't takin' any chances, not with a phantom what could spook a horse like Moon Dance. Close to where I'd left Head Toter I stopped and stood as still as a rock. I was good at doin' that, though I could never stop my heart from beatin', which some Apaches claimed they could do. I could slow it down though, so that's what I did, to keep it from poundin' so loud in my ears. Then I stood there rock-like, waitin'.

I didn't have to wait long. Down where Moon Dance and I had been surprised I saw the big shadowy blur pokin' around. He was bent over inspectin' our old camp, carryin' the headlike thing in one arm now and makin' noises what sounded like grunts and gurgles. With his other hand he was rakin' and pawin' the ground, feelin', I supposed, for our tracks. A good tracker can tell a lot of things about you just by feelin' the tracks. But the trouble was, he wasn't doin' it like a good tracker or even for that matter like a human bein'. He was sniffin' more than he was feelin' and after a little while he wasn't doin' other than sniffin'. Made you feel a little funny to watch him. He held the headlike thing in his hands like it was a part of him, and I had a feelin' he knew he was bein' watched. I've had such feelin's myself. When that happens your movements ain't so easy and loose as they was before you felt the eyes.

Close as I was, he still looked like a gray shadow blendin' soft into the night in the way some bugs takes on the color of the leaves and rocks around them. I had to keep my focus a little away from him so as not to see double, which I didn't want to do, 'cause if there's anything worse than one phantom it's two phantoms.

I closed my eyes for a moment to bring up my vision and when I opened them he wasn't there. It was as if he had blended totally into the night.

I felt myself shiver, the same instinctive sense of danger that Moon Dance must have felt. The little hairs at the back of my neck was bristlin' like a dog's, and those beneath my knees was doin' the same thing. My senses was tellin' me to get away. I couldn't tell how he'd got there, hearin' no noise at all, but I knew that now he was standin' in back of me and watchin'. I could feel his eyes.

I didn't move. No Apache ever moves in moments like that, no matter how much the little hairs under your knees is bristlin'. I waited. It seemed a long time. I don't think he was more than ten feet away, and if he was movin' I didn't hear him. In fact, there wasn't the tiniest noise in that whole vast night until I heard a kind of slow shufflin' already well down the trail from me. It sounded like some old Apache woman goin' barefoot to the spring.

I let him go, my curiosity now givin' way to a kind of respectful bewilderment. Phantom or not, he would've made a good Apache.

10

Headin' for Enemy Territory

MUCH AS I needed it, I didn't get much sleep that night. Thoughts of head-totin' phantoms kept goin' through my mind mixin' with thoughts of gun-totin' outlaws what would shoot you on sight and with thoughts of Apache trackers you knew was there but couldn't see. For a man who likes to know where everybody is and what they're doin', I was beginnin' to feel a little uneasiness of the spirit.

Early the next mornin' while the dew was still on the grass I coaxed Moon Dance back down the trail to where I'd last seen Head Toter. Some of his odor must've still been around, 'cause even before we got there the horse started shyin' again. At the place of our old encampment I got down to make an inspection. I found my tracks and my horse's tracks but I couldn't find any other tracks. I didn't know how, but that phantom wasn't leavin' any tracks. A head-totin' phantom was bad enough, but a head-totin' phantom what wasn't leavin' tracks was breakin' all the rules.

I was just turnin' away, still marvelin', when I saw somethin' that caught my eye, and I knew then why Head Toter wasn't leavin' tracks. Somebody—an

Apache for sure—was coverin' them. Hangin' on a thicket of chaparral bright in the mornin' sun was a red cotton thread that could've come only from an Apache headband. I inspected it to make sure. It was Mescalero. Of course there was the possibility that my trackers had left that thread there on purpose as a message to other trackers or to mislead me, but I didn't think so. It looked like bunglin' to me, the same kind of bunglin' made by a man what would shoot his own toe off.

So I went to work seriously. I knew what I was lookin' for and about an hour later I found it—the soft print of an Apache moccasin that showed the form of a mangled toe. We called him Missin' Toe for what he'd done with his own gun, but actually there was pieces of the toe left and that made him easy to track. I always thought maybe that was why Old Wickiup kept him on as sheriff even after he shot his toe off, so everybody would know where he was and not have to worry about him while he was enforcin' the law. Farther along in the direction Head Toter had gone the night before, I found two other prints. And though I couldn't be sure, I judged them to belong to Fantail and Poop—two natural born little spies if there ever was. Now that I knew who my trackers were, all I had to do was lose 'em.

There was two ways I could do that. One was tedious and the other was dangerous. I naturally decided on the dangerous one, tedious things never much appealin' to me.

59

What I decided to do—the dangerous thing—was to circle Guadalupe Peak on the last part of Espejo's trail and then ride fast straight east to the Pecos River and into the flatlands of White Eye territory. That was the only sure way of losin' Missin' Toe and his deputies—'cause if there was one place that even an Apache sheriff wouldn't go in those days it was into the flatlands of enemy territory, no matter who he was chasin'. The great Apache uprisin' had only been over with about ten years and the Texans was still nervous. Also they carried guns, every last one of 'em.

Now as you know, I never underestimate my enemies. It's the only way to keep alive. I knew I wasn't welcome anywhere beyond the Pecos River, at least not as an Apache, so I decided to make some changes . . . the main one bein' that I would go as William Brodie, if anybody asked. That meant I not only had to look like him but I had to talk and smell like him, and Moon Dance had to look and act and smell like William Brodie's horse. Since I *was* William Brodie I didn't worry as much about myself as I did about Moon Dance, who was much too beatuiful and intelligent ever to pass for a White Eye horse. And our smells worried me a little too. White Eyes say they're strong. I could always cut off some of my hair and put on boots, if I could find 'em, instead of leggin's, and Moon Dance might even let me put a bridle and a saddle on him, if I could find them too. But I didn't know what to do about our odors. I guessed I'd just have to take my chances.

Two nights later I rounded Guadalupe Peak, havin' followed Espejo's trail to the end. I knew the terrain now and most of the varmints infestin' it. All I had to do was lose my trackers and head into the mountains for Dead Man's Gulch and the gold. By now I figured I knew how to get there. I'd prob'ly run into all kinds of trouble, and surprises too, but I was bettin' I could handle 'em.

A coyotero moon was big that night I headed east for the Pecos and enemy territory. It was past mid-summer and the mountain valleys was dry and parched. Also some of the natural springs had dried up. Anybody not familiar with the country or in the company of a good horse might easily have died of thirst. Many men have perished that way in those parts. I wasn't worried about that. Moon Dance would find the water. And I wasn't worried about food either, 'cause as long as there's a quail or a rabbit alive, no Apache worthy of the name will get hungry, and there was plenty of them. I rode hard, not botherin' to cover my tracks. I knew my trackers would follow me till they ran out of mountains to hide in, then they'd turn back and set up camp and wait for me—forever if they had to.

The moon was high and I was slopin' down out of the mountains towards what's called the alkali flats when I saw the dyin' fire of an encampment in the distance. It was a little like the Apache gods was on my side in my attempt to find a pair of boots for myself and a bridle and saddle for Moon Dance. But even the Apache gods don't give you things for free or make things too easy for you. So I rode in cautious-like, the breeze in my favor, hid Moon Dance under a clump of tall mesquite and then slipped in close on the downwind side.

The fire was just about burnt out and back of it a ways laid two men with their heads on their saddles and their hats pulled down over their eyes. Their hands were clasped across their chests and in their hands each held a gun. It was Griz 'n' Cis, now armed again and dreamin' of gold. And they was snorin' loud enough to keep all the rattlesnakes in Texas at a respectful distance. They had a little melody goin' with the snorin', Griz goin' up high with a blubber while Cis came down with a kind of whistle. What with a coyote howlin' in the distance, it almost seemed the three of 'em was practicin' a tune.

What I did next I don't like to do unless I have to—steal. If I got to though, I figure it's better to steal from a thief than from an honest person. But before I set about to steal the boots, I noticed somethin' wrong. There was three horses staked out and one of 'em was Tied Up's. I guessed that accounted for the pistols, unless they was carryin' spares. But Tied Up wasn't anywhere around, tied up or loose. So I decided that since I was gonna do a little stealin' anyway, I might as well also steal a stolen horse. A real White Eye horse might come in handy. If I got in trouble with any Texas sheriffs I could always get on the other horse and say that Moon Dance was a mustang what I had run down and caught in the mountains. I didn't know any Texas sheriffs but I figured they'd believe me.

Stealin' the horse was easy, but gettin' the boots off a sleepin' man was gonna be a problem. Still, I had to have 'em. I only knew one white man what ever wore Apache leggin's outside of Apache society and as you might suspect, somebody shot him by mistake. My tradin'-post jeans was white man's jeans, as was my denim shirt, but I had to have boots too—too big or not—to pass for William Brodie, after of course I'd trimmed my hair a little with my knife and scrubbed my face good. White Eye kids, I'd noticed, unlike White Eye outlaws, are always clean.

I couldn't see if they was sleepin' with their boots on or not. Prob'ly was. Outlaws are always ready to run. I once heard of an outlaw what slept on his horse, but one night he went to sleep and fell off and broke his neck and the horse spooked and drug him the rest of the way to his doom, which couldn'ta been very far I guess.

The snorin' was louder now and the moon had dropped down a little and the coyote had left off his part of the song. I moved in a little closer, still thinkin' how hard it must be to get the boots off a sleepin' man without wakin' him up. They didn't seem to be the kind what would wear socks either, which was gonna make things worse. I could already begin to imagine the smell, which would prob'ly make me sneeze. And with those guns pointin' at the stars, and prob'ly cocked too, I mighta been pressin' things just a little even for a good-luck man. But I guess not only my luck but also my medicine was good that night. I got in close and was just beginnin' to work on Griz's boots, holdin' my breath against the smell and keepin' out of line of the pistol, when I noticed that Cis wasn't wearin' any boots. He had kicked 'em off and was sleepin' like a baby—a dirty baby—in barefoot peace.

Cis had the biggest feet—enormous and filthy—but I took the boots anyway. The two outlaws never once stopped their rise and fall of whistlin' and blubberin'.

Oh yes, I took the pistols too.

11

Buzzards and Dry Rivers

TIED UP'S HORSE, which I named Big Mistake, was just like his master, unhurried and uncareful. It took me three days to coax some Apache caution into him. By the time I'd done that we'd almost reached the Pecos River. That was deep in enemy territory and now I was not only an Apache in disguise, I was a horse thief too. They'd string you to a tree for stealin' a horse in Texas in those days, even if the horse you stole was already a stolen horse. I don't know where they'da found a tree, since I hadn't seen one for two days, but I suppose they had one around somewhere for such purposes.

I was travelin' only by night now, under a wanin' coyote moon. My trackers, Missin' Toe and his deputies, had turned back, which didn't mean they'd given up and forgot about me. Apache trackers don't do that. They'll track you forever if they been told to, and by now I was sure Old Wickiup had given them their orders, which was somethin' I couldn't quit bein' puzzled about. But then Old Wickiup always did do strange and complicated things, after which he'd blame everything on the Apache gods by sayin' they moved in mysterious ways.

One mornin' just before dawn, me and my two horses reached the river. It was dry, but with a little diggin' in the soft sand I managed to bring up enough water to satisfy the three of us. River water ain't the best in the world, bein' a little brackish and containin' wigglin' things, but if you're thirsty you don't notice it too much. I was just liftin' my head from drinkin' when I saw the buzzards.

They was high up and makin' big turns, which meant that their victim, whatever it was, hadn't died yet but that they was sure he or it was goin' to before another day dawned. And they was prob'ly right. Buzzards almost always are. They don't gather like that unless they're pretty sure of havin' a feast. I've fought 'em off old horses what was not yet dead, my love for dyin' horses bein' greater than my love for hungry buzzards. What's always amazed me is how they can be so sure the man or the beast they're followin' and circlin' ain't gonna make it. It must be somethin' about the odor.

The country they was circlin' over was flat and sandy with nothin' much on it but sagebrush and bulltongue cactus. There bein' very few places to hide, even from a buzzard, I began to feel for the first time that I was truly in enemy territory. But I was gettin' used to the boots I was wearin' and the short hair and in general feelin' more and more like William Brodie, native-born son of Texas. From time to time I'd call myself Bill just to see how it sounded. But what I really figured would make me a non-suspicious character was the two guns I had slung over Big Mistake's saddle, which was the style of all men in that part of the world in those days, young and old alike. Even some of the women wore 'em.

I spent my first day along the dry river hidin' in the tamaracks and willows along the bank while the buzzards made their turns overhead. By the time evenin' came they had grown in numbers and was dippin' always a little lower, though I figured they'd wait until the next day before startin' to do their pickin'. I could tell from the center of their circle about where their victim was, and when darkness settled down over the plains I eased out of my hidin' place to take a look. The buzzards had gone to roost somewhere by that time, prob'ly on the tall mesquite and sage, there bein' no real tree limbs around.

The moon was just risin' when I got to where I figured the buzzards' prey was. I was goin' moonlight-soft, not takin' any chances, and I was usin' the wind to my advantage, leavin' the rest to Moon Dance. It wasn't long before I felt his quiver, a gentle one, not the El Lobo kind or the Head Toter kind but a kind of curious quiver what might've been taken for sympathy. Even Big Mistake's ears went forward. I left the horses there and went the rest of the way on foot, first takin' off my boots, they bein' too big and not made for sneakin' up on anything. I had a feelin' I'd find Tied Up, dyin' of thirst prob'ly. But when I got in close where the person I was lookin' for was sittin', pretty well gone I could tell, I saw that it wasn't Tied Up or anybody else I knew. And I saw another thing. He was wearin' a metal star on which the moon was glintin'.

I slipped up beside him. He was moanin' a little, hurt I guessed, half-dead of thirst and prob'ly sun crazy too. I guess he knew he couldn't make it no farther and he'd been watchin' the buzzards and maybe that made him moan even more. It wasn't a pretty sound. I'd heard old Apaches make that same soft noise when they thought they was dyin' against their will, which they seldom do. Apaches don't die until they've made up their mind to.

I went back and got Big Mistake and brought him up. By that time the sheriff, if that was what he was, had stopped moanin' and was curled up against a clump of sagebrush. For a moment I thought he was dead, but then I felt him move a little as I unburdened him of his two pistols. It don't take much strength to pull a trigger: even a dyin' man can do it. I've seen 'em.

It took me quite a while and I had to do a lot of draggin' and pushin' and heavin' but finally I got the sheriff across the saddle onto Big Mistake's back. Dead and dyin' men, I've noticed, always seem heavier than live ones. The sheriff wasn't dead but he sure couldn'ta fought off any buzzards. Now they was gonna be disappointed, 'cause I inspected him for wounds and didn't find any, and there's not an Apache alive what can't revive a dyin' man if he's just sun crazy and dyin' of thirst.

Actually I've always thought I'da made a good medicine man, knowin' as I do the secret of what best brings a dyin' man back to life. It's the depth of his desire to live. Of course a little water helps if you're sun crazy and dyin' of thirst like the sheriff was, but all the water in the world won't do you any good if you don't want to live. He was wantin' to live bad, the sheriff was. Almost anybody with just a little knowledge of medicine could've saved him. You could tell by his groans that he'd do his part if the medicine man did his. There musta been an outlaw somewhere what he hadn't yet caught and he wasn't gonna die until he did.

I moved him and the horses back to the tamaracks and willow brakes along the river. It was good concealment, and, so long as we didn't have one of those big thunderstorms what often come on the plains, we wouldn't have any trouble. A flash flood, the kind they have in those parts in summer, would've drowned us— horses and all—and buried us too, in mud. But I had no choice. If I was gonna bring that old man around I had to get started. I was afraid he might lose hope.

His determination was great, but he needed a little willow tea and maybe a peyote button to make his pulse beat faster, and later on some jack rabbit stew. I didn't dare put any of that Pecos River water I'd been diggin' up out of the sand for myself and the horses into his system, at least not without bein' boiled.

If you want to kill a man dyin' of thirst just give him too much water too quick, and if you want to kill him fast give him Pecos River water straight—unboiled, that is.

I made a little oven affair in the sand that kept the flames from showin' against the night. You can be mighty careful when you have to, and I knew I had to, what with a lot of firearms and a stolen horse and a half-dead sheriff on my hands. Actually I guess I had two stolen horses and a pair of stolen boots too, but I didn't figure Moon Dance counted 'cause he was an Apache horse and I don't think anybody, even a Texan, would've considered Cis's boots worth sendin' you to jail for.

By the time the stars was blazin' full, I had got the sheriff's big white mustache soaked up with hot willow tea and he was lickin' at it with little brushy sounds. There was a lot of stained tobacco juice on the mustache too which the willow tea blended in with. I was boilin' my water in the old Apache way of usin' hot stones in a container, the container in this case bein' the sheriff's hat. I don't know whether it was the tea or the tobacco juice but he was eased some and after a while he went to sleep, makin' little moans of contentment. At first light I snared a rabbit and made a hatful of broth. It was intended for the sheriff, but me not havin' had a hot meal in I don't know how many moons, I had myself a fine feast out of the first hatful and gave the old man a few more sips of willow tea, a little greasy now from the remains of the stew. He had drunk about half of it when he kind of gagged a little, shook some of the froth from his mustache, opened his eyes and said, "Put up yer hands. Yer under arrest."

I guessed his mind was still a little muddled.

"Put up yer hands, Cactus Jack. Yer under arrest fer murder 'n' killin' 'n' thievin' 'n' robbin' 'n' mayhem 'n' disturbin' the peace."

That old man sure didn't need any peyote to put fire in him. He was comin' back to life fast. There was a wild light in his eye.

"I'm takin' ya in, Cactus Jack, and the judge's gonna hang ya from the tallest tree in Pecos. You've killed yer last man 'n' widdered yer last woman. Put 'em up."

I tilted his head back and tried to give him a little more greasy tea, which got no further than his big droopin' mustache with the dried discoloration of tobacco juice on it. He may still have had the cud in his mouth, 'cause when he spewed it back at me the greasy tea was streaked and flecked with somethin' more substantial than before. 'Course it may have been old chunks of dried sweat from inside his hat, which I hadn't taken much care to put in perfect cleanliness before usin'.

Now my problem wasn't so much revivin' him as it was holdin' him down. His eyes, blue and bright, was blazin' with a desire to get up. I guess he was still a little sun crazy. It takes some time for that to wear off. Fortunately he was too weak to move much, so I eased him back against Big Mistake's saddle and opened his shirt a little to let the mornin' breezes in. He went to sleep again then and I noticed where I'd opened his shirt that he bore a lot of old bullet and arrow scars. One of 'em, a lump in the shoulder, looked like the lead was still in there. And another one, kind of jagged, looked like the bullet or maybe the flint had been cut out by somebody not too qualified. They didn't seem to bother him none, at least not at the moment. He was sleepin' as peaceful as a drunk man, tobacco juice and tea and greasy soup and sweat still drippin' from his mustache.

I guess my medicines had saved him.

12

A Killer Storm

MR. SHERIFF, AS I'd now got into the habit of callin' him, out of respect for the law, kept up his peaceful dozin' through the rest of the day there in the shade of the tamaracks and willows. Havin' a little time on my hands, I took the opportunity to round out my ribs a little with some of the foods I'd been missin' while on the trail. With the sheriff's hat, which was about the size of a small barrel, and a few heated stones, I cooked up a lot of tasty Apache niceties, startin' out with a little more jack rabbit stew, then brazin' a partridge and finishin' off with some mescal sauce which I shared with my patient that evening. After a meal like that I was good for another two moons of slim pickin's. And it appeared, along about sunset, that I'd soon be back on slim pickin's whether I wanted to or not.

The sun didn't set properly that evenin'. It was a misty and dusty sunset, of a color and kind that always brings not only ugly weather, which is bad, but also ugly luck, which is worse.

That night the stars was pale and the air was strange and the horses was nervous. Somethin' was comin' for certain. Horses don't make mistakes about the weather.

And sure enough, the next mornin' the sun rose dull and misted over. It was all I could do to keep Moon Dance and Big Mistake under control. Both of 'em was snortin' and pawin' the earth and rollin' their eyes. They knew as well as I did that we was all in the wrong place, along a dry river bank, for the kind of storm what was brewin' somewhere in the mountains. They also knew about the kind of hailstones that fall. And as far as you could see in all directions there wasn't a shelter big enough to hold a man, much less two men and two horses and one of the men what still looked like he might have to be dragged. Even the buzzards had disappeared.

Horses, at least Apache horses, are supposed to get nervous when danger's in the air, but Apache men ain't. Old Wickiup had taught me long ago the disasters that can come from nervousness. He had showed me how cattle run over cliffs to their deaths and how even birds knock their brains out against mountains when they panic. That kind of thing, he said, was unworthy of a human bein', by which of course he meant an Apache Indian and nobody else.

I wasn't gonna panic. I knew that many men had died like that, runnin' blind out onto the flat plains in an attempt to find shelter when there wasn't none. I wasn't gonna start runnin' until I at least thought I knew the right direction. Then, when I'd made up my mind, I'd run like hell and take my chances, which was about as much as you could do. If I'd been by myself or in any other place than where I was I wouldn'ta

felt too much concerned, but I had to get the sheriff
and the horses out with me. One thing was certain
about that dry river: it was the most dangerous place
of all to be. When the storm broke in the mountains
the water would come rollin' down like waterfalls
from an ocean. The only warnin' you got would be
the thunderin' rumble of the river just before it
drowned you.

The sun had died in the mists now and the whole
land had got almost as dark as night. You could feel it
comin'. And like I had heard the White Eyes say about
approachin' disasters, it was gonna be damn bad.

I kept my calm. I always do, even when my instincts
is tellin' me to run. I had to get the sheriff ready if I
could. So I boiled up some stew for him, puttin' in a
few slivers of meat to give him more strength and addin' a little pinch of peyote to fire him up. He was
awake now and no longer quite so addled. I was sorry
I had to feed him with my fingers from his own hat but
he seemed downright grateful, gruntin' kindly like.
His eyes looked good too, and he didn't start ravin'
about Cactus Jack or other notorious fellows of his
acquaintance. Instead, he just looked up with those
keen blue eyes and said softly, "I'm much obliged to
ya, son. Where's ma guns?"

I gave him his guns.

He was comin' around fast. I knew the stew and the
peyote helped, but in truth I think it was his guns
what made the strength flow back into his body. He
had barely got 'em on and pulled 'em out of their

holsters and checked the chambers and spun 'em into place and whacked 'em back than he said, "Storm's a brewin'," and started gettin' up. Yes sir, I swear it was them guns what got him on his feet.

I helped him. He was wobbly but he was up. I gave him his hat and he set it on his head without even noticin' the drippin's, buttoned his shirt, straightened his star, polished it a little with his sleeve, hoisted up both guns again, patted 'em gently and said, "Let's ride."

Then he fell down, me catchin' him just before he hit the ground.

"Blasted legs," he said.

I held onto him. He was cursin' a stream now and spittin' too, mad at his blasted legs as he called 'em for not supportin' him, his blue eyes blazin' like fire and the mustache quiverin' with what I guessed was pure rage. I didn't pay him no mind, figurin' a sheriff's got his right to privacy like anybody else embarrassed by infirmities. Instead, I steadied him up and left him alone and went and got Moon Dance and Big Mistake and started helpin' him, still cursin' and spittin', up on the latter. I hoped he didn't mind ridin' a stolen horse.

In the saddle he did pretty well, his support not dependin' on his legs. I tied Big Mistake's reins together and hung 'em over his neck. The sheriff was grippin' the saddle horn with his big bony hands and cursin' a whole passel of people, Cactus Jack foremost among 'em. He stopped only just long enough to dig out a plug of tobacco and bite off a big chew, sayin' as he spat the fine juices in the air, "Ain't got time to make it to Pecos, son. Where ya figger on takin' us?"

"Leave it to me," I said, very confidently.

Actually I should've said, "Leave it to the horses." It was them what was gonna save us if we got saved. This time I was puttin' my faith in Big Mistake, 'cause if there's one thing a White Eye horse can do well when he has to it's find White Eye shelter. I think they can smell barns the way an Apache horse can smell enemies.

I told Mr. Sheriff to hold on. Then I whacked Big Mistake on the rump. He had free rein and he headed straight south with a thunder of hoofs that made you think he was runnin' straight for a manger to stick his head in. The sheriff was bouncin' high but holdin' tight, cursin' and spittin' in the wind, which had risen to an ugly howl.

Now the clouds had blackened everything and sand was blowin' hard against my face. I couldn't see much of anything but I could tell that Big Mistake either knew where he was goin' or had gone loco. He was runnin' with the wind and payin' no attention to sand dunes or mesquite or sagebrush or dry gullies or anything else. The sheriff was bouncin' pretty high at times with lots of space between him and the saddle but still holdin' on and still spittin' and prob'ly still cursin' too, though I couldn't hear now for the roar of the wind. I just hoped Big Mistake didn't hit a gopher hole and break a leg or maybe his neck. That would've been the end of him and the sheriff and maybe me and Moon Dance too.

The lightnin' and thunder started then and the first drops of rain began to hit. They were big and splattery and cold and meant we'd have a lot of wind and then a lot of hail and then if we survived there'd be more rain. I could already tell that this was gonna be what the Apaches calls a killer storm. No matter what happened, we had to keep runnin'. I wasn't worried none about Moon Dance. He'd run forever if I asked him to. But I wasn't sure about Big Mistake. He was carryin' a bouncin' load and runnin' too hard, not easy and good like an Apache horse. I figured him good for about an hour at the most. Then he'd go down and the sheriff'd go down with him.

While them thoughts was comin' and goin' the storm broke hard around us with the first big hailstones whackin' down. Moon Dance laid back his ears and Big Mistake put on a wild burst of speed. The stones kept crashin' down for what seemed a long time and then they passed and a cold rain started fallin' in tentfuls. It was blowin' on the wind and I could barely keep the sheriff in sight as he bounced up and down ahead of me. Then the thunder and lightnin' started crashin' around us again, so close that you could hear the fiery hissin' of the lightnin' bolts as they hit the ground and streaked across it. I remembered how I'd seen whole herds of cattle killed by lightnin' like that and whole mountains of trees burnt out. And while I was rememberin' them things the hail started again harder than before and this time I knew it wouldn't stop until it had killed everything it hit. I knew then it didn't much matter whether Big Mistake could keep the pace or not. With hailstones like that, all of us— horses and men—would go down and lay there squirmin' and twistin' and not able to do nothin' about it 'cept maybe curse.

I had just about made Apache resignation to a kind of dirty little death out there somewhere in enemy territory when I saw Big Mistake disappear into the blackness up ahead of me as if he'd run straight over a cliff. Then I felt Moon Dance slow up hard and quick with me slidin' all the way up to his ears. And the next thing I knew we was inside a big dark barn and the hail was hammerin' on the roof and the sheriff was half fallin' and half slidin' off his horse and still cursin' his blasted legs and you could smell musty hay and wet manure and harness leather and wet horses and oats somewhere and a kind of wet odor which only wet outlaws give off. I knew I was right about the odor when I saw the sheriff leanin' against Big Mistake all aquiver from runnin' and the sheriff aquiver too and holdin' a six-shooter in his hand and pointin' it at some shadowy forms of horses and men in one corner and sayin', "Lift yer hands, Cactus Jack, or I blast."

Cactus Jack lifted his hands.

13

Chickens in the Coop

THE SHERIFF HAD to shout to make himself heard
against the hammerin' of the hailstones on the roof.
Actually I don't think Cactus Jack even heard him. He
just saw the sheriff's big six-gun pointin' at his mid-
parts and he raised his hands as if he was used to doin'
it all the time. I knew how weak the sheriff was and
that he would've fallen down if he hadn't been leanin'
against Big Mistake. The trouble was, Big Mistake was
a mass of horsely tremblin' from that terrible run he
had made and was about to fall down himself. So I set
on Moon Dance listenin' to the hailstones on the roof
and got ready for what I knew was comin' next.

I still had Griz 'n' Cis's guns, one in each boot and
both loaded. Shadow-soft I eased 'em out. When Big
Mistake's tremblin' got so violent that he lifted a fore-
leg like a worn horse will always do and the sheriff's
support gave out and he sank down kinda slow like, I
saw Cactus Jack and the other three outlaws start to
make their move. I said, "Don't."

Just to put some force in the word, I shot a hole
through Cactus Jack's wet Stetson.

My shot made a loud noise in the barn, and though

Moon Dance didn't move a muscle, I thought for a moment that Big Mistake was gonna trample the sheriff to death. He was down under the horse's belly, floppin' around and cursin', the horse steppin' all over him. But I knew that bein' a real sheriff, he would rather be trampled to death by a horse than killed by outlaws, 'specially by an outlaw like Cactus Jack what seemed his special favorite. So I left him for a moment to his fate and told the gang to throw down their guns one at a time and slow. Then I fired another shot.

Cactus Jack speedily obeyed and the others followed.

Then I told 'em to turn around and not move or I'd get more serious in my law-enforcement duties, which I was beginnin' to enjoy. Only after I'd gathered up the guns—it was quite a collection—did I drag the sheriff out of the straw from under Big Mistake's belly. Other than wet straw in his face and damp manure on his backside he wasn't much damaged. His mustache looked bigger than ever with the straw stuck to it. I propped him up against a stall post and gave him his gun, which had got lost somewhere in the confusion. That strengthened him. The minute his horny old hand curled around that big revolver, he revived fast. It was as if his hand wouldn't work right unless it was grippin' a pistol. Seemed to have an effect on his whole body. I had to admit he was a tough old man. Where outlaws was concerned, nothin' could stop him. I had a feelin' he enjoyed chasin' 'em. And then I noticed that he enjoyed somethin' else—givin' 'em sermons about their evil ways. 'Cause he had just got his big hat on straight and his guns under control and his star wiped clean of mud when he started what seemed to be a speech. It was loud and powerful for a weak man.

"Evil-doers 'n' renygades, repent!" he shouted, spittin' some tobacco juice in the straw. "The Good Book says that if ya live by the gun ya'll die by the gun. An' may the Lord have mercy on yer soul, 'cause I've caught ya, Cactus Jack, and I see I've caught the Pecos Gang too, thanks to the Lord 'n' my deppity here." He meant me, though now I'd put my guns back in my boots since I didn't have any quarrel with Cactus Jack or the Pecos Gang.

"Evil-doers 'n' renygades," the sheriff shouted again, spittin' again too. "I ain't even gonna tie ya up, 'cause that'd deprive me of the pleasure of carryin' out the Lord's will by shootin' ya if ya try to escape, which I hope ya do. Just set down now 'n' take off yer boots and toss 'em in a pile and relieve yerselves of yer knives 'n' derringers 'n' other implements of destruction. And take off yer pants too if ya don't mind, though you can leave yer drawers on if ya got any, which I doubt. And then set yerselves down in that mud 'n' straw against the wall and pay no mind to the manure 'cause it won't smell any worse than you varmints already smell and we'll wait fer the storm to pass." Then he fired another shot through Cactus Jack's hat, which made shreds of the top part but which hastened the Pecos Gang along in the removal of their garments.

They looked just as sorry undressed as they did dressed. Cactus Jack's drawers, what had once been white but now was brown from dust and wear, was in shreds like his hat, which he still had on. And the other members of the gang looked as if their heavy underwear had more than once been used as a target for buckshot. If they'da had their guns on they wouldn'ta looked so unclothed and forlorn maybe. All a real outlaw—and these was real outlaws—has to take off to look complete naked is his guns. I guess that's why they looked so shabby in their underwear. It wasn't because they was drippin' water from their hatbrims and didn't have any pants or boots on and was sittin' in the straw like chickens, it was because they wasn't wearin' them revolvers.

"Deppity!" the sheriff said.

That of course meant me.

"Deppity. Yer lookin' at the notorious Pecos Gang. Evil-doers 'n' renygades. Robbers, killers, disturbers of the peace and committers of mayhem." He spit some juice in the straw and softly said, "Would you kindly help me to arise?"

He was still sittin' where I had propped him against the post. Now he had a big gun in each hand and was wavin' 'em around kinda careless-like. I helped him up, careful to go at it from behind him so as not to get in the line of fire if any of the chickens moved.

"Thank ya, kindly," he said. "Now let me introduce the gang." He was standin' wobbly-like and pointin' his pistols at each man as he introduced 'em. "That's

Cactus Jack, of course. And the other varmint is Cold Eyed Luke. Them other two ugly ones is Memphis Bill 'n' Dalhart Ike. There's another member of the gang, Three Finger Doc—I shot two of his fingers off one time in El Paso—but he ain't here. And there's a girl too that rides with 'em. She's called Sanatone Rose or Rosa Sanatone, dependin' on yer preferences. There's a song about her that I'd sing fer ya if I had a geetar. It ain't a bad song fer such a bad woman. I call her Sinful Rose. She reeks of sin. Maybe she 'n' Three Finger Doc got kilt in the storm. If so I'll bet even the buzzards won't touch 'em."

I knew the sheriff meant well and that he was a good man and tough and fearless and honest and upright and religious too. But for all that he was wrong about the storm killin' Three Finger Doc and Sanatone Rose, 'cause that old barn was big and it had a hayloft and the boards what was creakin' up there wasn't creakin' from the wind outside. The wind had died down and the hail had stopped and it was rainin' steady now. And though the sheriff didn't know and Big Mistake didn't know, I knew and Moon Dance knew that Three Finger Doc and Sanatone Rose was up there waitin' for the right moment to get what the White Eyes calls the drop on us.

I had to take some precautions. Though the sheriff was gettin' along in years and this would prob'ly be his last big ride against murderers and thieves and what he called evil-doers and renygades, I was young with many moons ahead of me. I had a whole lifetime of things to do—not the least of which was to find Old Wickiup's lost treasure for him so he, like the sheriff when he got the gang back to Pecos and had them hangin' from a tree, could die in peace.

14

More Chickens in the Coop

THE SHERIFF WAS in the worst spot possible. When you're dealin' with outlaws and killers like Cactus Jack and the Pecos Gang it's best not to stand against a stall post with your back to the hayloft door. 'Course I had put the sheriff there in the first place but that was what you might call emergency measures in time of deadly peril to keep him from gettin' trampled to death. Now I had to get him out of there. I didn't want him to get killed just before he had realized the ambition of his life, which I'd decided was bringin' in the Pecos Gang.

Now the boards in the loft could be heard creakin' louder in what seemed a most unnatural way. I noticed that Moon Dance was quiverin' a little too, sensin' that somethin' was wrong.

"Sheriff," I said. "Can you walk?"

"Damn betcha I kin walk, Deppity. And if I kin't I kin crawl. And if I have to crawl to Pecos to take this gang in, they're gonna crawl right ahead of me. I'll crawl 'em right up to the gallows tree. By the way, we got a good one, Deppity. Ever seed it?"

"Sheriff," I said, low as possible, "would you mind crawlin' over here?"

"What the hell fer, Deppity," he roared, spittin' and wavin' the pistols. "This is a good post to lean on."

" 'Cause if you don't, I gotta crawl out in front of you and shoot that guy in the loft what's gonna shoot you any minute now."

"The hell ya say!" He looked up. "By God, Deppity, I do believe yer right, as usual. I'll bet old Three Finger and Rose is both up there. Two more chickens in the coop!" He was mighty pleased at the thought of Doc and Rose bein' up there. "I'll burn 'em out. I'll set a torch to ol' Doc's tail. It's what the devil's gonna do to him anyhow one of these days," he said. Then he fired a couple of shots up through the planks by the hayloft door.

The thought of takin' Doc and Rose in with the rest of the gang so excited the sheriff that he forgot all about his weak condition and started surveyin' the rafters and the door and the ladder and firin' off a shot now and then for no reason I could see 'cept maybe the joy of it. While reloadin' his revolver he called out threats to the planks above, havin', I thought, not much respect even for the ears of a sinful lady.

"Deppity," the sheriff said, gettin' real spry now and cursin' all over the place and limpin' around lookin' up at the hole and steppin' in manure and mud and not noticin' a thing, "Deppity, I got to give ya an order. Would ya mind scootin' up that ladder 'n' stickin' yer head through the hayloft door to see if they is really up there?"

"I got a better idea," I said, not wishin' to get killed.

"Loan me your hat."

"Prob'ly too big fer ya," he said, takin' it off with the end of the pistol barrel and handin' it to me with the barrel pointed at my nose.

"I ain't gonna wear it," I said.

"I trust ya, Deppity. I trust ya. Whadda ya got in mind to do?"

"I'll show you."

It's a good thing I had boiled the stew and paralyzed the Pecos River vermin in the sheriff's hat before I went up the ladder, 'cause when I put it on a pole and stuck it slowly up through the hole, it got hit with so many bullets that it wouldn't 've served even for a fishin' net.

"Yep, they's there all right," the sheriff shouted, firin' a round or two himself. He was—I believe the word is—ecstatical. "They's up there all right. Step lively, Deppity. Step lively. We'll burn 'em out. Ya got any matches?"

"Matches won't work, Sheriff."

"Why not?"

"The barn's too wet."

"Then we'll smoke 'em out. That wet hay'll smoke good. Nothin' like it."

"Can't do that either, Sheriff."

"Why not?"

"They might have innocent persons up there, holdin' 'em as hostages."

"Deppity, ya think of everything. They might at that. Wouldn't wanta hurt any innocent people," he said, firin' a shot through the planks. "Whadda ya say we do?"

"Leave it to me," I said. "I got a plan."

"Blessin's on ya, Deppity. Blessin's on ya." And he fired off another one. The shootin'est sheriff I ever saw.

The storm was over now and though the afternoon sun outside was shinin' bright, the barn was still drippin' water through the rafters. Cactus Jack and the others was settin' on the mud and straw in their undergarments facin' the wall, lookin' around only when the sheriff fired off one of his shots to see if maybe he was gettin' too careless with his aim. When he quit shootin' they turned back around, lookin' exactly like wet chickens shiverin' in the coop.

I gave a glance to my surroundings. The old barn was built like most old barns. Cuts Plenty Throats had one almost like it in his pasture on the reservation. This one was big and high and had a slopin' roof runnin' down over the stalls and grain bins almost to the ground. I went out through a window of one of the oat bins, takin' a gun from my boot as I went. Where the roof made its slope to the ground the shingles had rotted and blowed away, and then I saw that the whole roof was in the same condition, so I had to be careful to keep my feet on the timbers. It looked like there was more holes than shingles. Also I had to take off the boots and put my Apache leggin's back on, leggin's bein' the only thing to use for walkin' on a rotten roof.

I wasn't doin' what I like to do best, which is to say

that I was takin' chances of gettin' shot. All Doc had to do if he heard a noise above him was to fire and I'd be back down on the ground where I started, with the difference that I'd prob'ly be dead. But I guess some of the sheriff's foolishness had rubbed off on me by that time, so I went slippin' up the steep roof until I reached a fair-sized hole among all the little holes in the rotten shingles. I had the sun at my back, so I took care not to throw a shadow over the hole. Except for the rotten shingles, it wasn't too bad a position, 'cause if Doc looked up, which I was afraid he might do, he'd get a blindin' glare from the sun. Even in foolhardy situations, I like to have the odds a little in my favor.

I laid flat on the rotten shingles for a while, listenin', my gun in my hand. They, the rotten shingles that is, smell awful, by the way, and the rotten little splinters tear your belly up somethin' awful. When I'd decided where Doc and Rose was, I eased up and peeked through a crack, keepin' a little distance between me and the big hole. They was down there, half hid in the hay, just their heads stickin' out. It looked like the sheriff had scared 'em a little with all his shootin'.

I lifted my gun, leaned over the big hole, and when I cocked the gun with my thumb it made a sound like a chain rattlin' in an empty room. Rose and Doc looked up out of the straw and I said, "Throw down yer guns or yer dead," usin' a little of the sheriff's tone and language in my command.

There wasn't much else they could do 'cept maybe hide their heads in the hay, which I suppose would've been mortifyin' for any member of the notorious Pecos Gang. So they tossed out their guns. Actually I don't think either of 'em knew for sure where I was. I had taken 'em by surprise.

"Crawl down the ladder," I said.

Bein' a gentleman, Doc let Rose go first, then he followed after. I hoped the sheriff was still there and still on his feet. Just to make sure, I waited until I heard his curses and commands and then I got down fast before his joy caused him to fire a few shots of celebration up through the rotten shingles. He never missed a chance to fire that gun.

Back on the ground I stuffed my leggin's into the toes of my boots, put the boots on and went back through the bin into the barn.

The sheriff had the undressed men sittin' facin' one direction and Rose sittin' facin' the other, so there wouldn't be any embarrassment. He was deliverin' a sermon on the evils of sin and how them what practiced it was gonna pay for doin' so. I didn't listen too close to what he was sayin', it not bein' meant for me and havin' heard it before anyway. And there was another reason too. I was listenin' to a noise comin' from a manger, a kind of muffled noise.

While the sheriff continued to preach to his congregation I went over and looked into the manger. There, tied up with a lariat, was a man. He was wearin' a clean white hat and a string tie and smilin' pleasantly, as best he could that is with a bandanna stuffed in his mouth.

15

I Hear Me Mentioned

REGARDIN' HUMANS, I got my likes and dislikes like everybody else. And like everybody else I don't always know why I like or dislike somebody. I just do. It's a feelin', instinct I guess. Now take Tied Up for instance, whose real name I now knew was John Sutler. I liked him from the first, if for no other reason than he was the only real civilized man I'd met since I left Mescalero Town. Bein' civilized in those parts meant of course that he was gonna be tied up most of the time and robbed regularly and prob'ly dead shortly. And it also meant that he was gonna be insulted and abused along the way. But despite all that, he still managed somehow to remain calm, cool, civilized and even—I don't know how—clean.

Now as I cut him loose and ungagged him he smiled real friendly like and said, "*Gracias, amigo.*" Cool. Civilized.

That was his way. Easy. No hurry. No bother. And he always seemed to be as considerate of you as you was of him, though it was you who was always untyin' him and savin' his life. Real cool. Real civilized.

"*De nada,*" I said, takin' on his easy ways.

"You got a haircut," he said, gettin' out of the manger and glancin' around at Rose and the gang and the sheriff and his own stolen horse as if all of it was the normalest thing in the world. His string tie wasn't even unstrung; it wasn't even twisted. How he did it I don't know.

"I got your horse back," I said.

"Thanks. Griz 'n' Cis again. I was on foot for a while." He smiled at that too as if it was the naturalest thing in the world for Griz 'n' Cis to be takin' his property every now and then and that he'd have to wander around on foot out there in the wasteland. But somehow I couldn't fancy him as buzzard bait. Beneath his casual ways there was some hint of another and not so helpless man.

"*Buenos Dios*, Sheriff," he said. "Looks like you cleaned out the western half of Texas."

"Me 'n' the deppity," the sheriff said, stoppin' in the middle of his sermon to the sinners. "Who tied you up? I'll prosecute him for impedin' the movements of free citizens."

"Don't rightly know, Sheriff. They got me from behind. It was too good a job for Rose and too bad a job for Cactus Jack. He's tied me up before and he ties good. I guess it was Three Finger Doc. His knots are always bad ones."

"The knot I put around his neck's gonner be a gooder," the sheriff said. Then he went back to sermonizin' his little congregation on the evils of sin and the price you pay for its commitment.

Tied Up interrupted him. "Why don't you just take 'em in, Sheriff. You can't reform 'em."

"Nope, but I kin try. I'll take 'em in when I'm done with my preachments. I been chasin' this gang fer twenty years and now that I got 'em and they kin't git away I'm gonna set right here and relieve my scars of all the aches 'n' pains that pack has put in my body. And if one of 'em makes a move before I'm through, I'll blast him."

"Is that justice, Sheriff?"

"Nope," the sheriff said, spittin', " 'tain't. 'Tain't justice at all. Justice is sump'n that they don't understand. But it's life in West Texas. That they understand."

"I see your point," Tied Up said. "And now if you'll excuse me, I got to be movin' on."

"Where you goin' with my horse?" the sheriff asked.

"Sorry, Sheriff. Old Blister's mine."

"Is that right, Deppity?"

"That's right, Sheriff. I stole him back from the men what stole him in the first place."

"That was good work, Deppity. I'll see that ya git a bonus fer it. That horse saved our lives and I'm grateful."

"Would you loan me a gun, Sheriff?" Tied Up asked. "Somebody took mine."

"Take as many as ya want," the sheriff said. "We got a whole arsenal."

Tied Up took Three Finger Doc's two pearl handlers, sayin' that they was the prettiest of the lot and that besides Doc never had put them to their best use anyway with those missin' fingers. Then he got up on Big Mistake, thanked me again in that cheerful way of his and turned to go. I gave Big Mistake a gentle pat on the neck to let him know he wasn't such a bad horse after all even though he wasn't an Apache horse. And as Tied Up was ridin' out through the barn door the sheriff stopped his sermon long enough to say, "Watch out fer rattlers, Sutler. The hills is full of 'em. 'Specially around that Apache gold. I'm goin' in there someday 'n' clean things out. You remember what happened to Brodie and his kid."

"I've heard," Tied Up said. "But I've never been convinced. Just because Brodie and his boy didn't come back doesn't mean the Apaches killed 'em. Maybe Brodie found the gold and took it straight to the Denver mint. One good horse could carry enough out of there to retire on."

"Nope," the sheriff said, spittin' big. "I seen his horse when it come back to Pecos. Had the Apache sign on it. You know what that means. It was the work of that crazy old chief. Someday I'll go git him and make him confess."

"Brodie had two horses, Sheriff. And besides, Apaches don't kill kids. What do you figure happened to the boy?"

"Don't know," the sheriff said. "The Apaches prob'ly took him along and raised him as a heathen. Another good Christian soul gone to hell fer sure. If they wasn't over there in furrin territory I'd go find out."

"It's only New Mexico, Sheriff."

"That's furrin territory." Then the sheriff said, "Deppity, give them varmints their pants but not their boots. I figger we can make Pecos by sundown. By the way, did I ever swear ya in, Deppity?"

"No sir," I said.

"I'll git around to it later. Now give 'em their duds."

I passed out the pants. The outlaws started stumblin' around in the wet straw and manure puttin' 'em on, cursin' low and growlin' at the sheriff, who didn't pay 'em any attention except to spit in their direction. Rose set kinda prim-like to one side, pickin' her teeth with a straw and hummin' a little tune which wasn't, I don't think, a hymn. Tied Up was movin' off, which I was sorry for. There was a couple of questions I wanted to ask him. I had a feelin' he knew who I really was, but I didn't worry too much about him gettin' lost from me 'cause next to the sun or the moon, he was the easiest thing to follow that ever existed. He was lookin' for the gold and I was lookin' for the gold, though prob'ly for different reasons, and it was certain that our trails would cross again before either of us found it, even if I had to arrange the crossin'.

Right now I had to arrange my departure, and I had to do it in a way what wouldn't cause any embarrassment to the sheriff, who'd gone back to preachin' against sin for the benefit of his evil-doers. He kept right on preachin' steadily while gettin' the outlaws on the horses. Since there was only five horses —I guess the outlaws had lost one somewhere—and there was seven people, countin' the sheriff, there had to be some doublin' up. The sheriff of course reserved a horse for himself not only for safety's sake and for dignity but also for transportin' the weapons and boots. Then, bein' kind and considerate towards ladies, he gave Sanatone Rose a horse for herself and made the five outlaws double up. The sheriff never stopped his sermon all this time and the outlaws never stopped jawin' and cursin', which only made the sheriff curse back and preach a little louder. When I'd finally got him on his horse along with his mound of guns and boots, and stuffed his feet into the stirrups, he drew himself up tall in the saddle, fired off a few rounds from his gun, and cried out, "March!"

The raggedy little procession started movin' off slowly into the sunset.

I mounted Moon Dance and rode the other way.

16

Everything Is Beautiful

THERE'S SOME THINGS it's best not to think too much about if you want to keep your wonderment alive. In my case at that moment in my life one of those things was myself, by which I mean how the Apaches came to find me in the first place and what happened to my father and whose sign was on that horse that returned to Pecos, and about a thousand other questions that had troubled my mind in the summer-soft and winter-bitter moons of my childhood days. Everything that had ever bothered me about myself was beginnin' to fall together, and I was afraid that if I thought about it too much I might fall apart. That would've been a very un-Apache thing to do. And if there was one thing I now knew, for sure, for better or for worse, as they say, and for eternity too prob'ly, it was that I was an Apache Indian. And I didn't want to be anything else.

I couldn'ta been. I woulda been what the Mescaleros say is neither a bird or a bear, what the White Eyes calls a mess. Bein' an Apache, all Apache, maybe not pure but all, I could feel the endless wonder of bein' alive and free every moment of my life in a clean-sweet world of stars and mountains and deserts. Even the storms, the big thunderstorms, was beautiful. I was as poetical in my earth-sweet love of livin' as Old Wickiup when he sang his songs, though I hoped for my sake I'd never be as crazy.

Apaches are, I'd come to learn, strange and beautiful creatures, not so much for their looks as for their ways. If an Apache don't want somethin' to exist, it don't exist. It's one of the secrets of the tribe, which, along with the horses, has been the cause of their survival. An Apache can make almost anything vanish from his mind forever, startin' with his own name. As far as he's concerned it's no longer there and in its place he puts somethin' what he likes. From the time he's born he learns to do this, and by the time he dies, which he also does after his own fashion, he's had nothing but a lifetime of beautiful thoughts in a beautiful world, no matter how harsh and cruel it might seem to a stranger.

I guess my white blood really didn't have much effect on me as a human bein'. Everything that ever went naturally through my head went through in the Apache way. I had their instinct for survival and I always relied on it when faced with what a White Eye would've thought was a hopeless case.

So now I rode into the night, free again and un-burdened with White Eye complications. I now knew one more secret about myself and I was afraid to think too much about it. Instead, in pure Apache fashion, I put William Brodie away and became again the Good

Luck Man, Arizona Boy, Arizona Slim, or whatever I wanted to call myself—tall for my age, wise for my years, and once again Apache-happy with my life.

I had my horse and I had the stars. I had lost my trackers long ago. Now I could head for those ghostly mountains—the Guadalupes—and find Old Wickiup's gold.

Everything was beautiful.

Later that same night when Moon Dance and I had made camp along the first slopes of the Guadalupes, I felt that everything was perfect, which to an Apache means that everything is normal. About halfway through the night, while I was pickin' out the stars in the Mexican sky and thinkin' how truly fine in life it is to be a good-luck man and untormented by all the foolish things what un-good-luck men look for and die for and never find, I heard the distant trample of horses goin' fast. You could tell by the sound that there was four and that they wasn't bein' spared or takin' precautions of any kind. They was runnin' hard through the star-soft night in the direction of the Rio Grande, keepin' to the edges of the hills.

I mounted Moon Dance and rode out to a high mesa to take a look. There, unseen, I watched them ride by below, four shadowy horses runnin' crazy through the night, two of 'em carryin' a double load. I didn't have to look to know that the men was bootless and prob'ly gunless too and that the woman—actually I think she was a lady—had a name so pretty that a song had been written to her.

And I knew that somewhere back there in the alkali flats there was a sheriff a cursin' and a spittin' and a shootin' off his pistols at the stars. And prob'ly deep down inside he was happy about it all, 'cause now he could lay awake nights and dream of bringin' in the notorious Pecos Gang. Dreams is good for old men.

I have said that everything was beautiful, which it was, and I have said that everything was perfect, which it also was. But there was still one mystery which I had to resolve before my mind would settle down to what the Apaches call the easement of the spirit. To do that I had to find Tied Up.

That would be easy.

It took me about an hour, early the next morning. He was cookin' himself a rabbit for breakfast, makin' enough smoke to roast a steer. It looked like he was sendin' smoke signals to somebody in Mexico. I caught him by surprise. Just as he turned around, a piece of rabbit in his hand, I said, "What about her?"

He didn't even blink. For all his easy ways, he would've made a good Apache. I had a feelin' maybe I didn't take him by surprise, that he was actually expectin' me.

"She is dead."

Apache-like, he didn't pronounce the name.

"And she was?"

"Apache."

"Mescalero?"

"Maybe. Maybe Mimbreño."

"Tell me."

It was almost pure Apache talk now. He put the rabbit down.

"He came from Oklahoma. Indian Territory. She was already dead. He had you and a map and two good horses."

"Did he find it?"

"Yes."

"And then."

"And then they killed him."

"They didn't kill yours."

"He didn't find it."

"The letter said he did."

"He wrote an untruth. Boasted."

"Why?"

"Didn't want people to think he'd wasted his life. He came close, but he didn't find it."

"What about the nuggets?"

"Everybody's got nuggets. They're scattered all over West Texas. A lot of men have found that gold but he didn't."

"Did any get out?"

"Don't think so." For the first time, he smiled. "Do you think you'll find it?"

"I've got to."

"I won't ask why."

He was good in Apache ways. From the start he hadn't broken one civilized rule of Apache conversation. No foolish questions, no needless talk, and most important no namin' the dead.

"Do you want the map and the letter?"

"No. You keep them."

Then I smiled too. "Do you think you'll find the gold?" I asked.

"No," he said. "But I don't have to."

"*Adios*," I said.

"*Adios*," said he.

And now I could go with an easy spirit. I knew as much as I could hope to know and certainly as much as I wanted to know. She had been an Apache, maybe even a Mescalero. Her hand had drawn the map. Now I was freed from the puzzlements of all my youthful years, my mind unburdened and my Apache soul in peace.

My feelin', as usual, rubbed off on Moon Dance. He wanted to run through the mist-sweet mornin' for no reason but for runnin'. I let him. It was as if him and me was both runnin' away from a world that neither of us understood or wanted. It was almost as if we was runnin' back to those mountains and a time before any conquistadors had come to seek the Mescalero gold.

"I've got to find it," I had said. The words rang in my ears, beat in my blood. "I've got to find it."

And I knew I did. In my very soul I knew I had to find that gold. It wasn't just so Old Wickiup could die in peace. Knowin' him, he couldn't 've died any other way. Bein' a pure Apache, he could convince himself that the gold was found even when it wasn't, and die as happy as an eagle in its flight, which, come to think of it, he sometimes resembled. It was somethin' else, somethin' I felt in my spirit. I had the feelin' that some gentle breeze—pure and sweet—was blowin' there. I had never felt a breeze like that before. It seemed to be carryin' away a lot of old confusions that I no longer needed, like the name William Brodie. I would never use that name again. It would cease to exist. I was now a pure Apache. The tribe was me and I was the tribe. The way I now felt about the gold was tied to somethin' goin' clear back to the beginning of the tribe in the Guadalupes, somethin' what made them the keepers of a secret that had outlasted all the conquerors and their descendants, somethin', actually, which they didn't even need, or want, or use, 'cept maybe for an occasional trinket to decorate a horse. It was as if they had lost everything on earth to the invaders except what the invaders had come for in the first place, what the invaders really wanted, the only thing—the gold.

That meant that the invaders, though they had invaded, hadn't conquered, and that so long as the gold was safe there might just as well have never been an invasion . . . 'cause the rest didn't count, despite the blood and tears. The Apaches could stand the blood and tears—they had whole mountains of 'em, a black rock for every tear—but they couldn't lose the gold. When they lost that, the conquistadors had conquered. And conquerin' meant the spirit—the Apache spirit—was gone forever on the desert wind.

That was why I had to find it.

Moon Dance ran. I let him run. He could, I think, have run forever, so long as he was headed west, away from the White Eye world.

I never cease to marvel at the good sense of horses, especially Apache horses.

17

Through Dead Man's Gulch

FROM THAT MOMENT on I had but a single mission, like Padre Glorio at the reservation church used to say. But mine was tryin' to save Apache gold instead of Apache souls. I hoped my mission wouldn't be as long and hard and fruitless as Padre Glorio's. Apache souls, for some reason, are awful hard to save.

I now knew the terrain and what you might call the local population. My impatience to find the treasure was kept under control by that cautious side of my nature which always insists that I come out alive.

Whoever finds the gold of the Guadalupes must die.

Just to make sure the legend didn't apply to me, I swore an Apache oath not to take any unnecessary chances—not one.

I was now doin' what I do best, what I sometimes think I was born to do, by which I mean that no tracker on earth, not even an Apache tracker, can follow me if I don't want him to. I can say without fear of braggin', that I'm the best eluder what ever eluded in the whole Apache world. 'Specially when I know the terrain and all the livin' creatures in it. From then on it's mostly a matter of the senses, of seein', feelin', listenin', smellin', and a lot of watchin' and waitin'. That was one reason I followed the old Espejo trail around the mountains in the first place. My senses just don't work at their best until I know every sight and sound and smell and bush and rock and bird and beast around me.

And there was another reason for followin' that trail too. It was what you might call for the benefit of the ignorant, like Lobo and Head Toter and Winchester and maybe Griz 'n' Cis. I figured they might think I was goin' in after the gold from that direction and also think that if I didn't know the right direction to go in from I wasn't worth botherin' with, which in their way of thinkin' meant I wasn't worth shootin'. That was all right with me. I never have liked the idea of bein' shot at by madmen, 'specially from behind and close up.

But it wasn't El Lobo and the others that I was mostly worried about; it was Missin' Toe and his sneaky deputies. Sooner or later, I knew, they'd pick up my trail away from the Pecos River and then they'd start stalkin' me, patient and tireless and serious. And when an Apache tracker starts stalkin' you like that, it don't matter how good you are at coverin' your trail or how sharp your senses are. You got to be careful.

And so there now began for me the most patient and careful deceits I ever worked in my life. Though Dead Man's Gulch was only about a two-day ride ahead of me, I was prepared to spend the rest of the summer gettin' in there if necessary, so that when I finally did get there I would not only be the only livin' human there but also the only human on earth what knew I was there. That's what you call playin' it safe, at least from men. I was discountin' rattlers, they bein' less dangerous where gold's concerned.

In the usual Apache way, I didn't pay any attention to time. Days and nights, if you start countin' 'em, can cause you to lose some of your patience. As far as you're concerned they don't exist. I don't know how long I stayed in hidin' at the place of the Blue Mound, which is where I headed west for Dead Man's Gulch. It might've been two days or it might've been two weeks. I do know that it was long enough to satisfy me that no livin' soul was followin' me and that no pumas or mountain cats was stalkin' me either. If a cat stalks you a man can stalk the cat, and another man can stalk the first man and so on. When finally I moved on it was on a moonless night with the breezes comin' at me from the mountains. I had to know what was ahead of me as well as what was behind. And I didn't take a step without coverin' my trail with every art known to an Apache. Maybe I even invented a few.

Deep into the mountains the goin' got rougher. At times I had to put rocks back in their place where Moon Dance had disturbed them with his hoof. If he accidentally chipped one, I patiently smoothed it down with sand until you couldn't tell it had ever been touched. We was both walkin' most of the time, the trail narrowin' up here and there with big drops on both sides. It was rough and dangerous terrain, 'specially at night. One slip would've sent you over the side of a cliff. I knew there was a leveler and easier way in to Dead Man's Gulch but I also knew it was more in the open and I was keepin' to the oath I'd taken not to let a human eye detect my presence. Dangerous mountains was one thing, but dangerous men was another.

One of my problems was water. It wasn't easy to find and when you found it you had to be careful not to leave any traces of havin' been there. Trackers always pick around water holes, tryin' to find some horse slobbers or grass what's been disturbed. Moon Dance wasn't the kind of horse what slobbered, and if he trampled any grass I took care to put it back in shape before we left. I watched for buzzards too. Buzzards sometimes come pokin' around just to see if what's movin' down below is healthy or not. A good tracker watches them almost as close as they watch him. And then there's the eagles and owls and other birds. No matter how careful you are, they're gonna squawk if you disturb 'em, and then they're gonna rise straight up, usually right over your head. Every step in them mountains is a dangerous one when you're tryin' not to be seen or heard.

That was the way I passed my days and nights, how many I don't know. Just before startin' up the last part of the trail to Dead Man's Gulch, I went into hidin' and backtracked on foot two nights in a row just to make sure that no one was behind me. Once I went through Dead Man's Gulch there would be no other way out, 'cept for Suicide Leap higher up in the mountains. So I backtracked, makin' one last check. Everything was fine. I didn't find a soul or any evidence of a soul. Once I thought I heard the faraway sound of what might've been a shot, but it was so distant and faint I decided I'd been mistaken. Havin' been on the trail so long, I figured my senses was maybe a little on edge and that I must've been imaginin' things.

Early the next mornin' I went up through Dead Man's Gulch and continued on until I found myself lookin' out over a mesa green with grass. I had made it in.

And I felt good about it 'cause I'd done it like a pure Apache. No man or beast or bird had laid eyes on me.

Or so I thought.

'Cause right then Moon Dance whinnied and tossed his head back in the direction of Dead Man's Gulch.

Whoever finds the gold of the Guadalupes must die.

My amazement was total.

No tracker on earth—Apache or otherwise—could 've found or much less followed the trail I had laid down with such patience and care. I had passed over that whole wild region without leavin' so much as a speck of my passage. And that included Moon Dance's turds, which I had collected and dried and scattered like pollen on the air. I hadn't disturbed a rock or a twig or a creature of the earth or a bird in the sky. There was only one answer to the mystery—the wind.

Scent.

I had used the wind to know what was ahead of me,

backtrackin' to cover my rear, and someone or somethin' had used the wind just like I had used it, keepin' my scent and backtrackin' with me. Apaches were good trackers, I knew, but they couldn't do that. Only an animal or somethin' with an animal's nose could've done that. Also Moon Dance had caught the warning scent against a gentle mornin' breeze, which meant strong odor.

Strong odor.

An animal or something like an animal.

Head Toter.

I stood dead still, my hand restin' on Moon Dance, feelin' for the quivers which didn't come now. The strong odor had vanished. Now my puzzlement was less but my uneasiness more. It wasn't that I was afraid of phantoms or whatever Head Toter was. And it wasn't that I was scared of that head or whatever it was he always carried with him, though I was gonna keep my distance from it. It was because I knew that if Head Toter could follow me, somebody else could follow him—Missin' Toe and his deputies.

Whoever finds the gold of the Guadalupes must die.

It looked like the legend was tryin' to come true.

I hadn't found it yet, at least not to my knowledge. And then while I was standin' there as still as a lizard on a rock and feelin' for Moon Dance's quivers and wishin' I could get just a hint of my stalker's location, I caught a glimpse of a crevice droppin' down beneath some great boulders at the edge of the grassy knoll not a rattlesnake's strike from where I was standin'. I looked directly at it. It disappeared, blended with the earth. I turned my head slowly to the right and back. There it was again.

I did not move one muscle.

But I knew I had found the gold of the Guadalupes.

18

Night and the Phantom

I KEPT MY CALM. I always do when my life's at stake. Nervousness can get you killed. The truth of the matter is, I was more fascinated by that crevice under the rocks than I was fearful of what was down the trail behind me, meanin' not only the phantom but Missin' Toe and his deputies. They was there for sure, and that meant trouble, but I couldn't quit marvelin' at the entrance to the gold long enough to worry about them. What caused me to marvel was, you couldn't see the entrance from any other spot but the one I was standin' on. One step one way or the other and it disappeared, blendin' right in with the boulders, scrub pine, grass and earth. If you even turned your head the least little bit it vanished. You could actually walk right over it and not see it. To put gold in a place like that was one of nature's marvels. To give it to the Apaches was another one. And there was still another marvel too: that Moon Dance had whinnied when he did. That whinny had stopped my foot in the exact and only spot from which the crevice could be seen. With such things happenin', I began to think that I at least had the Apache gods on my side, dependin' of course on whether I got out alive or not.

I marked the location in my mind, like an X on a map, takin' into account the shadows from the risin' sun and checkin' the position of every rock and tree around me, not even leavin' out the tufts of grass growin' around the boulders. I had the feelin' that once I stepped away from that spot I would lose that crevice in a deceptive play of light and rocks and trees and never find it again. It wasn't surprisin' that Old Wickiup had lost the treasure, and even less surprisin' that the conquistadors had never found it. The marvel was that some people had actually found it.

But I had no time to ponder the matter. I was standin' on top of the gold, and somebody—a lot of 'em maybe—was waitin' down the trail to see what I did next.

The sun was risin' high over the mountains now and I saw with some regret that there wasn't a cloud in the sky. I could've used a storm, at least some wind and rain, to cover my movements. But the sky was clear and clean and blue, what the Apaches calls a good-luck sky—a good day to fight battles and win, or, if you should lose, a good day to die. I would gladly have traded it for one of those blood-soaked sunrises when Apaches won't set foot outside their wickiups. Sooner or later that kind of day will bring wind and rain and lots of natural disasters. There's nothin' like a good storm to wipe out all traces of your tracks. It'll do it almost as complete as dyin'.

To tell the truth, I don't think the thought of dyin' actually bothered me as much as the thought of bein' caught by Missin' Toe and his deputies. That would've meant shame and humiliation, and there's nothin' worse. I would've been known forever as Man Who Got Caught or Man Without Brains or somethin' like that. I would've been taunted by little kids and made to do squaws' work. I just ain't—never was—made for that kind of thing.

I knew I was in a bad spot, without a gun or even a bow and arrow, havin' stashed 'em along the trail with Cis's boots. I knew I might not get out alive, but I also knew another thing. I was still alive and young and healthy and had my horse. That's all an Apache what won't humiliate needs.

Plus a lot of luck of course.

I knew what I had to do and I knew how I was gonna do it. I was takin' chances, sure, lots of 'em, but sometimes you got to. The phantom wouldn't come up through Dead Man's Gulch until he could do it in the dark. He only moved at night. That meant that Missin' Toe and his deputies wouldn't move until the phantom did, since they were trailin' him in their attempt to locate me. They wouldn't move until daylight came again, bein' Apaches and dislikin' the night.

I set to work.

What I did first was hard to do. I walked Moon Dance across the grassy knoll, leavin' tracks deep and clean, up to a rocky trail, then I backtracked him coyote style, each hoof print fallin' in the ones he'd made before, until we got back to where we'd started. It was a good job. That trail and both our scents disappeared on the rocks ahead, the tracks seemin' to go on up in the direction of Suicide Leap. Then, facin' the boulders and the scrub trees over the crevice, I jumped him into the thicket right above the spot where the gold lay hidden. He made it clean, without touchin' a leaf. Then I laid him down flat, dug myself a hole beside him and wormed into it. We couldn't 've been found unless you walked right on top of us. There was only one more precaution to take—blot out our odors.

There's lots of ways to do that and I knew 'em all. Skunk oil's the best, but I didn't have any. I guess that was an oversight on my part. Some Apaches I know carry it around all the time to use in emergencies. Horses, though, don't take to it too kindly. Moon Dance prob'ly would've objected. Wild herbs of the kind old Mad Woman used to use to kill the odors of cooked sheep with are good too, but they wear off pretty fast. And besides, there wasn't any around that I could see. Pine oil works good, 'specially in the mountain air. If you lay it on heavy it lasts a long time. So I worked my way over to the green scrub pine and tested the leaves. They was soft, rich with summer juice. It didn't take me long to blend Moon Dance's odor and that of my own into the clean mountain air of that good-luck day. After that even the phantom couldn't 've sniffed us out. Just to make sure, I laid on a hint of wild garlic that I found growin' out of the rocks. By the time I was through, we smelled like nothin' but an empty part of the forest. Now, if the rattlesnakes would just leave us alone, all we had to do was wait.

Patience was the important thing, and that's what an Apache's got plenty of. If you're patient, you stay alive. If not, you die.

Noon passed and nothin' happened. I didn't think anything would. The phantom wouldn't come out till night, and Missin' Toe and his deputies wouldn't move until the followin' mornin'.

Evenin' came and I rescented us with oil just in case the cool air brought out our natural odors. Still nothin' happened.

Later on the moon rose, what the Mexicans calls a Comanche moon—bein' good for raidin' across the Rio Grande—and then darkness settled down and the creatures of night came out. I recognized 'em all by their cries and sounds. Everything was normal, undisturbed. It was hard to believe that there was stalkers out there in the night, such was the calmness and beauty of everything in its place. If you hadn't known they was out there you wouldn't 've suspected it. Everything—the stars, the mountains, the birds, every livin' creature, was in its proper place and undisturbed.

I watched the moon, keepin' my eyes soft and listenin', not just with my ears but with my whole body, hearin' nothin' but the creatures and the leaves what was supposed to be makin' noises. And while I was doin' that, a strange thing happened. I suddenly remembered, out of the mists of my childhood I guess, that I had been there before, in that same spot, out there on the grassy knoll, playin' with a string or somethin' while some man—my father, I guessed—was down below in that hole under the rocks and pines I was usin' for concealment. The picture was clean and clear. It was the same picture I'd been carryin' in my memory since my childhood days. Quietly I looked at it, the grassy knoll, and as I looked I felt a strange soft sense of sadness and relief pass over me like a breeze. For one long and trembling moment I wondered if maybe I wasn't what the Navajos call moon-mad.

But I knew I wasn't.

I had been there. That was the spot where the Mescaleros had picked me up.

That vision, I guess you'd call it, had just passed when Moon Dance let me know by a low snort that the stalker was comin' closer. I gentled him, though he didn't need it, and gentled myself too. Then I felt an un-Apache shiver ripple over me, and I think Moon Dance shivered too. There in the moonlight, as if he'd dropped from the sky, not ten feet away, was the phantom—Head Toter, still totin' the head, or whatever the thing was.

19

A Kind of Sadness

FOR ALL MY shiverin', his grunts was more pitiful than frightenin'. It was the great gray blur arrivin' there like a ghost in the moonlight what brought the hairs to risin' on my legs and caused the ripples along my spine ... that and his sniffin', which was more like an animal than a human bein'. My odor had blended with the wild pines around us and he was now sniffin' around for tracks to follow. He got down on his knees, lookin' like a tired old bear in the moonlight, and then got slowly up again. His movements was made with an effort and seemed to pain him. After a few gurglin' sounds mixed with what sounded like spittle, he found the tracks and followed them across the grassy knoll until they played out along the rocky trail. For a long time he stood there, huggin' his head, the one he carried, as if it might break or get away.

My plan was workin'. Now he ought to sniff his way on up the trail and get confused and turn around and come back to where the tracks played out and then start circlin' up ahead on the trail again tryin' to pick up my scent, the way an animal would do. But after he had stood up there a while and turned his head this way and that several times, I saw that my plan wasn't made for phantom animals. Instead of sniffin' on up the trail, he turned and sniffed back along the tracks to the spot where I'd backtracked Moon Dance and made the jump. There he turned around a few times, growlin' and gruntin' and seemin' confused and lost and angry. And then, when I didn't expect it, he screamed such a high and splittin' scream that Moon Dance and I both bolted straight up. We were standin' right in front of him.

He just stood there, not movin', lookin' back at us, makin' a low gurgle now, and I decided to risk everything in that moment.

Actually it wasn't my decision. There just wasn't anything else to do. That scream had woke up every bird and beast and tracker in that part of the world. I had to do something, and the only thing to do was to lunge, bring him down with me, head and all if necessary. Then I'd decide what to do next. Carefully I judged the distance. And then, just before I lunged, another thing happened, in a way more startlin' than the scream. He looked straight at me and spoke one word, "Brodie."

I stood stone dead. The word had been so unexpected, and the voice had been that of a tired old man, a very tired old man, nothing animal about it.

"Brodie." He drew the word out long and slow.

"What is it, old man?"

"Brodie. You are John Brodie's ghost."

"No, old man."

"Here." He held up the head-like thing. "Put it back."

"Why, old man?"

"Because I'm going to die. I'm tired and I've lost the place. Take it back, John Brodie. Put it where it came from."

Apaches don't even like to mention the dead. To name them is taboo. When he held the head out I took great care to look past it and over it and around it but not at it. Instead I looked at him. He was old and bent and his odor was powerful. His face in the moonlight was nothin' but a blurry bush of whiskers with sunk spots where his eyes was. His hat, which looked as old as he was, was fallin' into shreds. I wondered how many rains and suns had poured and burned on him. While lookin' at him, I listened for the night things to quiet down around us, which they did. And that meant if Missin' Toe and his deputies was anywhere near, they wasn't movin'. I could thank the night for that.

"Go away, old man," I said softly.

He paid no mind. "I saw you one time before, John Brodie. I saw you die. You found the gold and the Apaches killed you."

"Speak softly, old man," I said. "And please don't speak the name you speak."

He paid no mind to that either. "Then I saw you ride into these mountains two moons ago," he said. "I looked closely at you and I knew you. You knew I looked at you. Your name is John Brodie and I saw you die and now I see you again."

"When did you see me die, old man?"

"Moons ago. I spied you to this spot, you and a boy. I saw you go down to the gold and I saw the boy at play."

"What happened to the boy, old man?"

"I did not see. Here." He offered me the head again and took a step forward.

"Who killed me, old man? Who struck the blow?"

"I do not know. One of the chiefs. Here." He took another step. "Here, John Brodie."

"Please do not speak the name you speak."

He grunted, still holdin' out the head.

We were close now, almost touchin'. Behind me Moon Dance was quiverin' a little because of the odor. I still couldn't break the Apache rule of handlin' human remains, so I looked over the head and asked, "Who followed you here, old man?"

"I do not know. I do not care. Here."

"What is your name, old man?"

"I do not remember."

"But someone did follow you here, didn't they, old man?"

"Many of them. One was shot. Maybe two. And I too am going to die. That is why you must take this and put it back where it came from."

"Why, old man?"

"Because you brought it out. You dropped it on the day you died. I picked it up and later I went down there. I ran away for what I saw."

"What did you see, old man?"

He seemed not to hear. "I tried many times to put it back, but I couldn't find the place. Then I saw you return. I knew you'd know the place. I knew what you had come for. Here."

He held it out again.

I looked down then at the thing. It was a chunk of solid gold.

"You're almost standin' on the place, old man."

He looked down and grunted, his words givin' way to gurgles again, as if he'd forgotten all about the ghost what had risen from the dead. Then he bent over and dropped the chunk of gold down the hole. It seemed to fall a long way before it hit. When I looked up he had turned and was paddin' soft along the trail towards Dead Man's Gulch. In an instant he had blurred into the night, on his way to die.

I stood there in the moonlight feelin' a kind of sadness and also feelin' Moon Dance's quivers fade away as Head Toter went shufflin' into the night. There was enough light for me to cover his tracks by, and not till then did I discover that he had wore no shoes. But it wasn't his tracks what worried me, for they was faint on the rocky ground and unshowin' on the grass and easy to cover; it was his odor, so strong that even a White Eye could've followed it if the wind was right.

I had to work fast now. Mornin' would bring Missin' Toe and his deputies and I didn't know how many others. They might even be movin' up the trail now, though I figured that unlikely. It takes more than a scream to get an Apache sheriff to do his work at night. I didn't let myself think about the fact that I was already cut off from any escape through the gulch. The reason I didn't want to think about that was that there wasn't any other way out except the cliff at Suicide Leap, and I figured it was rightly named. In other words, I was in a trap.

Trapped or not, I was goin' to do what I had to do. Feelin' as I now did, I couldn't do otherwise. There's times like that in every man's life, I guess. I was goin' all the way, riskin' everything. I was goin' to see this mystery through completely to the end, maybe the bitter end, maybe even the bloody end. I was goin' down that hole. I'd deal with Missin' Toe when I got to him, or maybe he'd deal with me, but I wasn't turnin' back. I put all thoughts of danger from my mind and went to work.

Long before the first bird woke I had Moon Dance hidden about two arrow flights up the trail and had returned to the entrance of the gold. I heard nothin' down towards the gulch now but I knew they was there, waitin'. They'd move when the light of day began.

Fifty feet down, the map had said.

Slowly, without leavin' a trace, I slipped feet-first into the hole. For a moment I hung there lookin' up at what must've been the last bright star in the sky and feelin' nothin' under my feet.

20

The Gold

FOR A MOMENT I had me some regrets that I'd not brought a rope, though that would've been as fatal as fallin' down the hole, maybe more so. 'Cause to use a rope meant you had to tie it to a stake or a tree, and my trackers would've found it quicker than a sidewinder can strike. All the luck in the world couldn't 've saved me then.

Then I remembered something. And it seemed so fittin' and proper and full of salvation too that I felt a kind of poetical tingle in my suspended toes.

I remembered Acoma, the sky city of the Pueblos, where one time I'd gone with Old Wickiup. There I had seen where the Zuñi had chipped away their handholds in the side of the mountain to use in fleein' from the conquistadors. Now, hangin' there suspended over the gold, it seemed to me most fittin' and proper and even a little poetical that I should use the Zuñi handhold system in makin' my descent.

Hangin' by one hand, I got out my knife. First I chipped out a toehold. Then I chipped a handhold. The cliff seemed to run almost straight down. I kept workin' away. It wasn't easy, but I was makin' progress. Soon I could start usin' the toeholds for hand-holds and the work went faster.

In a little while I was down out of sight and listenin' carefully between the chips for any signs of my pur-suers. I was relyin' mostly on the birds, which I could hear from up above makin' their first songs of the day. So far they was singin' undisturbed.

I must've been down about the length of an Apache war lance when I knew somethin' above me wasn't right. The birds had paused. I paused too, waitin', leanin' into the side of the cliff, my ear against it. For a long time I heard nothin' but the poundin' of my heart, which seemed to be tryin' to knock a hole in the side of the cliff. Then, there it was—the quick soft sound of Apache feet. I'd know 'em anywhere, even six feet underground.

They was bein' careful, I could tell. You would hear a kind of flutter of feet and then silence, a long silence, and then another flutter, kinda like a bird. They was doin' it Apache style, from bush to bush and rock to rock, stoppin', waitin', goin', stoppin', waitin', goin'. They knew they was close to somethin'. But I could tell from the circlin' and turnin' of the soft foot-flutters that they didn't know how close. In a little while I heard one go one way, one another, and the other one another. Now they was searchin', and doin' that Apache style too. They'd circle a while, then they'd be back, then they'd circle some more, lookin' for a sign, any sign that might tell them where I was. I hoped they didn't find Moon Dance, but I put that thought out of my mind, 'cause I'd seen what Apaches can do to horses what they don't want around.

The first rays of light found their way into the cave when I was down about another lance length. Patiently I worked my eyes in the shadows and made out what seemed a shaft of soft light about two or three more lance lengths down. I couldn't tell where that soft glow was comin' from but I was sure it was slantin' across the bottom of the cave. I was tempted to drop, but that would've been runnin' just one more unnecessary risk and I was already runnin' too many. So I went on with my chippin', listenin' for the pad of feet to return and hopin' they wasn't listenin' for me, and watchin' for rattlesnakes too, knowin' as I did their habit of gatherin' in cool places in the summer time.

What mystified me was that shaft of light at the bottom. I couldn't figure out where it was comin' from and why it was so faint. As the light outside got brighter the shaft below got bigger and glowed more. Slowly I chipped away. It wasn't until I was down to about a lance length from the bottom that I realized I wasn't lookin' at a shaft of light but at a great lode of pure dull yellow gold—Apache gold.

It was a kind of seam runnin' solid through the mountain, about the size of three or four big pine trees laid on top of each other. It came out of one side of the mountain and disappeared into the other. On all sides of the seam was broken pieces and nuggets of all shapes and sizes. I dropped down then, not even rememberin' to look for rattlesnakes. And as I stood there in a kind of shadowy glow of light lookin' at the gold which had so baffled the conquistadors and who knew how many others, I saw what no Apache likes to see, anytime, anywhere—bones, dead men's bones.

Whoever finds the gold of the Guadalupes must die.

I wished that sayin' hadn't popped into my mind like that, without any warnin'. And I wished the bones wasn't so close. Those bones was cursed, cursed by the legend. Those bones had found the gold, and the gold itself was cursed, and I was standin' there on top of it, dead men's bones around me.

And I hoped I didn't do what for a moment I thought maybe I would do—disturb those relics in the crazy hope of findin' some little trace, a watch, a ring, a paper with a name on it. I didn't. I turned my back. I already knew that if I got out of there alive it'd take me half the remainin' moons of my life to purify myself and maybe even then I'd carry the taint of the dead.

A little more light was comin' in now, or maybe my eyes was gettin' better accustomed to the dark. Keepin' my back to the bones, I took a look around me.

I was down between forty and fifty feet, I guessed, and I noticed that the side I'd made the chips in didn't run straight down, as I'd thought, but sloped slightly inward from the entrance so that if I now looked up I couldn't see any hole at all and if anyone looked down he couldn't see nothin' but darkness. The seam of gold, solid and pure—not quartz or rock gold but pure gold —ran straight through and across the floor of the cave.

There was no tellin' how far it ran after it disappeared into the mountainside, though I felt it safe to guess that no man, except maybe the remains of them I wouldn't look at, had ever seen so much pure gold all at once in the same place. You couldn't blame the Apaches for puttin' a curse on it.

Bein' an Apache, the gold itself didn't much impress me, but I got to confess that the sight of so much of it all at once was kind of staggerin'. I guess I had expected to find a lot of nuggets, and instead I'd found an entire mountain.

Walkin' carefully along the seam, the way you do on logs across a stream, I followed it to where it blended into the earth on the other side. There I sat down and dug softly with my knife into the earth. I was careful. I knew Missin' Toe and his deputies was above me somewhere, waitin', listenin', watchin'. Bein' Apaches, they'd wait right there until the three of 'em died of old age or they found me, whichever happened first. Sooner or later I knew they'd find Moon Dance, and when they got around to it they'd kill him and then hide somewhere and wait for me. Apaches can be cruel when they figure it's necessary. In that respect I doubt that I ever could be pure in my Apache ways, such is my love for horses. So I dug badger-soft, wormin' my body in above the seam. I was diggin' there 'cause the seam ran sharply up and I figured it might rise near to the surface somewhere after twenty or thirty feet. It was easy diggin', there bein' more earth than rock, and I had pulled out a lot of the earth which I was tempted to sprinkle over the dead in Apache respect for untended bones when suddenly I broke gently into another cave.

I stepped back, careful to stay hidden in the first cave. Then cautiously I peered up through the hole.

For a moment I was blinded, the sunlight passin' through a wide opening about twenty feet above. The seam of gold, I saw, had disappeared again into the earth, as if it had broke off just before goin' into the other cave. From the opening above the second cave or even from inside the cave you couldn't 've told any gold existed. I looked up towards the hole and the sky. And then I stopped breathin'. Passin' slowly by the hole was the shadow of a man.

Missin' Toe.

21

A Mysterious Hoot Owl

I NEVER GIVE UP. No Apache ever does until he's dead.

I wasn't in that bad a shape, at least not yet, but I was in about as bad a place as you can be and still be alive. My problem now was to stay alive. I didn't want to die until I could do it in the proper manner at the proper time and in the proper place. This was the wrong place and I was too young. And besides, my horse was expectin' me.

I watched the shadow closely. It was Missin' Toe all right. You could see by the form the shadow made that he was wearin' his big sheriff's hat and his six-guns and not much else in the way of body garments except his baggy Apache pants. Both as an Apache and a sheriff he looked ridiculous. I think it was the hat what did it. But ridiculous or not, I knew he'd stay right there without food or drink until I either came out or he was convinced I wasn't in there or that if I was I was dead, good and dead, as they say.

From the way the shadow fell I could tell it was the middle of the afternoon outside. There was nothin' I could do but wait for night. While waitin' I carefully filled up the hole between the two caves, smoothin' everything over so well you couldn't 've told any hole had ever been there. And all the time I worked, I kept my back to the bones.

By the time night came and I could hear the noises of distant creatures flutterin' down and diggin' in to rest, I had formed a plan. It was what I guess you'd call a desperate plan, bein' as it was the only possible one and much too dangerous for a man what had taken a solemn vow not to run any unnecessary risks. So I waited while the birds outside got settled down and the moon rose and everything on earth was in its rightful place, then I started back up the ladder of handholds I'd come down on. Once I got out I would rely entirely on my knowledge of the world of nature to see me safely through. If anything moved, I'd know it. And if anything wasn't in its natural place, I'd know that too. With my instincts and my luck and a lot of patience, those creatures of the night would give me all the help I needed. If there's one thing you can count on, it's nature—birds and bugs and owls and rattlesnakes and the like.

Slowly, quietly, I scaled the steep wall of the cave, like the Zuñi up the mountain in the lost moontime. Just as carefully I poked my head out of the opening, keepin' concealed under the bushes.

The night, the earth, the world was beautiful.

A moon was risin' and the stars was shinin'. I think, havin' been down there with the bones for so long, I could've got poetical about the beauty and the freshness of the world. But this wasn't the proper time and place for that either. So I just clung there to the last handhold, holdin' my breath and tryin' without success to stop the poundin' of my heart. I had one hand outside the crevice grippin' a scrub pine by the root. The rest of me was still inside. I had a feelin' that I was comin' out of a grave, which I guess I was.

My breathin' and heartbeat was hard for me to control. Both of 'em sounded loud, at least to me, in the stillness of the night. And both, I knew, could put my life in peril. Breathin' is enough to make a night creature like a cricket stop his song, and a beatin' heart against the earth will disturb a sleepin' snake. No cricket stopped though, nor did I hear any slitherin' of rattlers as slowly I eased up under the scrub pine. There again I waited, listenin', watchin', feelin' with all my senses. There wasn't one nerve of my body what wasn't atingle with excitement.

And it's a good thing, too, 'cause in that moment I heard the faint clear call of a mountain owl from up the trail about where I'd left Moon Dance. I was sure it was an owl, but my instincts told me to take no chances. Apaches can make the same hoot when they want to, and I don't think even an owl can tell the difference. And then I heard what my instincts told me I might hear, another hoot, this one almost right behind me. That was Missin' Toe replyin' to the hoot up the trail. Still I waited. And then, from down below Dead Man's Gulch there came another hoot. I recognized that one. It was Fantail. They was checkin' their positions—one at my horse, one at the cave, and one below the gulch.

The owls was quiet then for a moment. And then somethin' happened what shouldn't 've happened. Farther away than the first owl, up the trail somewhere far beyond Moon Dance, came a fourth hoot from an owl that was neither an owl nor an Apache. If it was, it was a sick owl or a sick Apache, maybe even a dyin' owl or a dyin' Apache, 'cause that hoot wasn't even close to the real thing. Nobody on earth could've told who or what it was exactly but it was somethin' or someone what wasn't supposed to be hootin'. Actually it sounded like a joke, bein' such a poor hoot and so unexpected. It was a startlin' thing to hear.

And I guess it startled more than me, 'cause right after that strange and mysterious hoot what didn't belong anywhere on earth that I knew of, I heard Missin' Toe do the one thing no Apache ever does unless he's completely taken off his guard—he jumped. It was a jerky jump, stoppin' almost as quick as it started, but it was enough to cause a whole flurry of creatures to shoot out of the trees and bushes, not to mention the rocks and grass. That was when I, instinctively, shot up out of the hole and came to rest behind a rock. By the time Missin' Toe had settled down and the flurry of birds and bugs had died away, I was in perfect concealment behind my stalker.

Now, at least for the moment, I had a slight advantage. I knew where my stalkers were and they didn't know where I was. In fact, I knew just about everything except who the fourth hoot owl was. I knew that Missin' Toe was right in front of me, not more than the toss of a lariat. I knew that Poop was up the trail waitin' for me to return for my horse. I knew that Fantail was down the trail at the gulch that I'd have to pass through if I hoped to get out alive. And I figured they had closed the gulch too by this time, so that even if I was lucky enough to get to my horse and then lucky enough to get out, I'd either have to fight my way through or find some other way.

The trouble was, there wasn't another way—except Suicide Leap. That was on up at the end of the trail and it was a thousand feet deep and I don't know how wide, and though there was nothin' on this earth Moon Dance wouldn't 've tried if I asked him, I somehow couldn't think of endangerin' that horse's life by askin' him to jump the cliff at Suicide Leap. When it comes to horses, I always get soft in the heart . . . and maybe in the head too.

I took a little comfort in the fact that they hadn't killed Moon Dance yet, and now I thought I knew why. They figured I might slip by them and go into hidin', waitin' for the right moment to whistle for the horse. When that happened they would close in. And if I then got away they'd force me up to Suicide Leap, put my back against the cliff, so to speak, and starve me out . . . though I knew that with my life at stake I could stand a lot of starvin'.

And so I had it all clear, except for the fourth hoot

owl, and since they didn't know who it was either, that made us even—almost even, only three to one, which for an impure Apache is pretty good odds even when up against two pure Apaches and one with a missin' toe.

22

Up to the Rim

EVEN AN APACHE'S gotta sleep sometime, though I honestly think I'm an exception to the rule. Missin' Toe, however, wasn't. About an hour before first light, I noticed a slight change in the air on the other side of the rocks from me. Things was too quiet. What had been a wide-awake body lyin' in wait for me had slowly—so slowly I almost failed to notice it—become a body deep in silent sleep. Missin' Toe had broke another rule . . . dozed off. Knowin' him, I wasn't too surprised. If all Apaches had been like him the race would've died out long ago. Any man what would shoot off his own toe ain't a reliable man. I just hoped he hadn't slipped into his sleep with his gun in his hand, 'cause I knew that if anything woke him he'd come up shootin'. If there was one thing I didn't need right then it was a lot of wild shootin'.

When I was sure he was asleep and not settin' some kind of a trap to trick me into movin', I set to glidin' sidewinder-soft over the rocks between us. I went slow, careful not to break the silence of the night. About two feet from him I saw him stir a little, shift his position against the rock, and suddenly wake up.

He shot to his feet and I lunged.

Behind me I heard a little flurry of wings and the startled sound of birds. Missin' Toe rose straight into the air when I hit him, his hat flyin' even higher. And then I saw him disappear hatless into the dark hole he'd been guardin', the hat seemin' to hang in the air for a while before it floated downward after him and out of sight. That was when the shootin' started.

Missin' Toe was shootin' with both guns, straight up through the hole. All around me the bullets was bangin' and the birds was goin' crazy. And then I noticed that Missin' Toe was shootin' too much even for him, and the shots was too evenly spaced. He was shootin' three times, bang, bang, bang, then pausin', then three more times. Signals, they was. He was givin' signals to his deputies. I feared the worst.

So I was runnin' then, faster than I'd ever run in my life, faster even, I was sure, than any human on earth had ever run, 'cause I knew my fellow tribesmen and how they ain't got one speck of feelin' about killin' your horse if they figure they got to. They'll even kill their own horse if they got to. I knew as I ran that even now Poop was movin' in on Moon Dance, that the long knife was out and ready and that he was whisperin' horse talk to a much too trustin' animal. I could've whistled and he'da come, but I wouldn't 've known then where Poop was. And I had to know that if I hoped to get through the day alive.

I ran.

I ran so hard I hurt, but still I ran.

Dimly I saw a little light around the peaks of the mountains, and a lot of things, wild and crazy things mostly, was goin' through my head, thoughts that scared me, thoughts I didn't want. So I blanked them out and kept on runnin', strainin', tryin' to fly, to reach that horse.

My heart leaped high as I saw Moon Dance up ahead of me, but it sank as I saw Poop reachin' out for him. One hand formed a twitch around the horse's nose, and in the other hand was a long and ugly knife. For a moment I think I tried to scream. I knew how fast an Apache can slit a horse's throat, and I knew what horses look like when they go down that way. Suddenly I felt a retching in my mouth and a shivering in my bowels, whether from runnin' or from somethin' else I couldn't tell.

I saw the knife go up.

I whistled.

Moon Dance reared high, Poop hangin' to his nose, the knife flashing.

I whistled again. Moon Dance struck with his hoofs and swung his powerful head. Poop lost his hold and hit the ground not a foot from me. He hit rollin', the knife still in his hand, and when he stopped rollin' he was runnin' down the trail.

I was tremblin' and I think Moon Dance was too, but he came trottin' up, snortin' and nose-nudgin' me in the backside with horsely affection and what I like to think was gratitude. Maybe even it was love.

But there wasn't any time now for horsely affection.

I still didn't know where that fourth hoot owl was or even who he was, and I knew I was cut off at the gulch. The sun was just beginnin' to rise and this wasn't gonna be no good-luck day. The sun was heavy and seemed to be drippin' blood, the very kind of day they say that Mangus Colorados met his doom. I could feel a foreboding in the air and I wondered if maybe my good luck was runnin' out just when I needed it most.

Moon Dance didn't seem to think so. I was hardly on him before he started dancin' up the trail in that lordly way of his, ears forward, head tossin', tail flickin'. But that blood-red sunrise worried me. It was goin' to be the kind of day what brings disasters. Addin' to my depression also was the fact that I was cornered and I knew it. There was now too many uncertainties. Who and where was the fourth hoot owl? How was I gonna ride through Dead Man's Gulch with three Apaches waitin' for me? And worse, I was goin' in the wrong direction—towards Suicide Leap, the rim of the earth.

Suddenly behind me I heard a bird, a startled bird. Instinctively I went to the ground, takin' Moon Dance down with me. Over my head an arrow cut beautiful and deadly through the air. Before it hit the ground I was up and Moon Dance was runnin', me holdin' the tail for three jumps and gettin' up on the third. I had no choice now. There was only one direction to run and that was the wrong direction. I ran, knowin' now they was comin', silent and sure, deadly in their intent, two of 'em prob'ly, leavin' one to guard the gulch.

Higher up the mountain, the trees growin' scrubbier now, I looked back. Nothin' was movin', but they was there, comin' on. I could feel it. Now and then a bird lifted and now and then I felt Moon Dance make that little quiver he always made when there was someone he could hear or sense but couldn't see. I pushed on, still higher. We was up in cougar country now, cougar and goat country, mostly rocks. I kept movin'. They kept pressin'. The slope upward grew steeper. I needed a gun, a bow and arrows, a lance, even a club would've helped, but I had none. I didn't even have the hope of holdin' out till night, 'cause that blood-red sun wasn't halfway up the sky yet. And where, I wondered, was the fourth hoot owl? Prob'ly up the trail waitin' for me, though I couldn't imagine why, 'cause that trail didn't go anywhere except to the rim of the earth. I could see the cliff of Suicide Leap up ahead of me now lyin' at the edge of a large grassy plateau. I guessed that was where the good-luck man would make his last stand.

And then I saw somethin' else there on the grassy knoll. A man. The fourth hoot owl. He had a rifle under his arm and a pistol in his hand and he was white and dressed in the style of a gambler and—by God I swear it—he was clean, spit 'n' spam, as they say, un-ruffled. I don't know how he did it.

23
Dealer's Choice

MOON DANCE WHINNIED and the world seemed brighter. Even that blood-red sun seemed to lose its drippin's of defeat. Tied Up motioned us in behind some rocks where we could control the grassy mesa, and then, like the Apache I think he was at heart, wasted no words on foolishness of any kind. It wouldn't 've surprised me if he'd started right out speakin' Apache. Cool? Other than Old Wickiup, I've never seen a man so cool in moments of desperation. I think he was enjoyin' himself.

"Dealer's choice," he said.

"Who's dealin'?"

"You and me."

"Pretty high stakes," I said.

"Makes the game more interestin'. We may even have to cheat a little."

"You don't hoot good," I said.

"Out of practice. I used to do it better."

"Where's your horse?"

"Somebody stole him."

He said it as if it was the normalest thing in the world, which by now I knew it was. It was almost as if his horse was supposed to be stolen, as if it couldn't be any other way, as if maybe he'd even planned it that way. All the time he talked he never took his eyes off the rocks down the trail, watchin' easily, casually, not missin' a thing. And all the time he watched, he never stopped smilin'.

"They don't know where we are," he said. "So I figure they'll just take their time and try to starve you out or make you try the jump."

"I'm not jumpin'," I said. "Too dangerous for my horse."

"I think he could make it."

"I want Missin' Toe," I said. "I want to take him back and drop him in front of Old Wickiup."

For just a flash I saw surprise in his eyes. It was as if he knew somethin' I didn't, as if he was sayin' "You're forgettin' somethin'." But he didn't say that. Instead he said, "Don't ruin it."

"What?"

"Everything." And before I could ask another question, he said, "That would make the odds too high against us. I like to keep 'em fairly even."

"You're the dealer," I said.

But I guess he sensed my puzzlement, 'cause while keepin' his eyes on the rocks down the trail he started talkin' again.

"It takes a while," he said, "for a young Apache to understand Apache games, especially the kind the old chiefs play. They're usually deadly affairs, most of them so complicated they don't make sense until the game is over and sometimes not even then. I imagine you've heard of Nana and I know you've heard of Geronimo. Both of them were masters. So is Old Wickiup. I know him and I think I know the kind of game he's playin'. It's for big stakes and you're in the middle of it. You might even get killed. That's part of the game. But there's one thing that you must know."

"What's that?"

"Missin' Toe don't count."

"That makes no sense—not even Apache sense."

"It will someday."

He stopped talkin' then, his eyes still on the rocks.

"All right," I said. "You're still the dealer. Let's get on with the game."

He waited a while, as if thinkin' things over, and then said, "Dead Man's Gulch is open."

"Fantail's guardin' it," I said, watchin' a bird rise up and knowin' that one of my stalkers was layin' out there waitin' as only an Apache can wait. They wasn't in any hurry now. They'd take their time. That was the Apache way.

"Fantail won't go near the gulch. The phantom is lyin' right in the middle of it. He died there the other night before your trackers got their horses through. Probably beginnin' to stink a little by now. And just below the gulch is El Lobo. He limped up there and died after Winchester shot him and Missin' Toe shot

Winchester. There'll be a lot of buzzards movin' in by now and in a day or two the mountains will be clean again. Look."

He was right. High up the buzzards was beginnin' to turn. As the day wore on they'd drop slowly down.

"What about Griz 'n' Cis?"

"I met 'em over in the flats," he said, without takin' his eyes off the rocks. "On their way to Pecos to buy a pair of boots, though I doubt if either of 'em has got that much money."

"It was the phantom," I said, "that ruined my trail, wasn't it?"

"Yep. He sniffed you all the way. You led him and he led the rest of us. It was a parade."

"There's lots of gold," I said.

"And how about the bones?"

"Lots of them too."

"How did you find the opening?"

"Pure luck."

"I hope it holds," he said.

Another bird rose. Otherwise the mountain was quiet. Far off the buzzards turned, swooping always a little lower. Tied Up was still smilin' that easy smile, the true gambler enjoyin' himself while gettin' his cards ready to play. I think he took things—everything —as if they was a game of poker and he couldn't wait to call the other fellow's hand, if for no other reason than to see what he was holdin'. Whether he won or lost was prob'ly not of any interest to him, though I had a feelin' he'd rather win than lose, 'specially when the stakes was so high.

We dug in a little closer behind the rocks. I laid Moon Dance down flat and made a good concealment for him. Neither of us, man or horse, had drunk any water for two days now and both of us needed a little wettin' of the tongue, as they say, but that would have to wait. Tied Up had a small canteen but he knew better than to tease a thirsty horse by openin' it. He also knew that an Apache and his horse can go for two or three times that long without water if they know how to conserve their energy. As long as you don't start thinkin' about it, you're all right. It wasn't the dryness of my throat what bothered me. It was the exact location of Missin' Toe and Poop. I guess that was what was botherin' Tied Up too, 'cause for a long time he didn't say a word, just set there clean and neat behind the rocks, watchin', waitin', listenin'.

Late that afternoon we saw the buzzards begin to descend, some of them dippin' down and out of sight. There was a lot more of 'em now, gatherin' for the feast. It wouldn't take 'em long, once they got started, to clean up the gulch.

Finally Tied Up said, "They're over there. Two of 'em."

"Are you goin' out with me?"

"Nope. Missin' Toe's not lookin' for me. If he shoots me, it's by mistake."

"He does that a lot."

"I know his reputation."

"How do we play the first card?" I asked.

"I think you're goin' to have to whistle," he said, meanin' for my horse after I had got behind my stalkers.

"They'll try to kill him," I said.

"I know. I've got that card ready too."

The buzzards kept up their turnin', descendin' faster now. That blood-red sun was beginnin' to fall now in what looked to me like the color of bad luck.

"This ain't a good-luck day," I said.

"We'll have a Comanche moon tonight. With a horse like yours and a Comanche moon, who could lose?"

He was right about the moon. When the buzzards had settled down to roost and the moon came up I was surprised to see that such a day of gloom could bring such a night of hope. Darkness came quietly and the stars were beautiful. It was a night like the one when I rode out of Mescalero Town. I hoped I would ride back before morning under the same bright stars.

"I know where they are," Tied Up said softly in the dark. "Take your time. Go slow. Before you whistle for your horse give one long hoot and wait for the echo to come back. I'll make a move over in their direction. Then whistle and start runnin'. I'll play all the cards then except the last one. That's yours."

"Meanin' gettin' through the gulch?"

"Meanin' not only that but the horse race that's gonna follow after you get through. That's why there's one waitin' on the other side of the gulch. He's got the horses."

"That's Moon Dance's card," I said.

"Does he know that?"

"He will when the time comes."

"Good luck."

But I didn't go. I waited, uncertain, not of the night or the stalkers or the cards or any of that but of something else. I looked at him. He was smilin', still enjoyin' it.

"Why?" I asked.

"It's simple," he said. "I like deadly games—with happy endings."

I slipped shadow-soft into the night before the moon was big enough to cast a shadow. He was right. These was deadly games. I couldn't yet say about the other part.

24

Under a Comanche Moon

I MADE SOFT thanks to the Apache gods what long ago decided that night was not the proper time for fightin' unless you absolutely had to. The way the Mescaleros see it, only crazy men, by which they mean White Eyes and Mexicans, fight at night.

I needed the night and I needed my luck. To slip by two Apaches ain't easy. I not only had to slip by them, I had to ask Moon Dance to run by them too, or maybe through them or over them, whichever way he chose. I think that's what I was prayin' to the gods about mostly, 'cause the memory of that knife was still fresh in my mind. The gods approvin' or not, I knew what I would do to Missin' Toe and Poop if they killed him. I would stalk 'em to the ends of the earth, not just the Apache earth but the whole earth. And the deadly games I'd play with them would have no happy endings. Old Wickiup had sent them after me, not after my horse.

Half an arrow flight from where I'd started I laid my ear to the ground. Everything was quiet. Only a faint slitherin' a step or two away. Rattlesnakes. They was nestin', unbothered and unbotherin'. Their soft sounds blended with the night, as natural and in place as the rocks and scrub trees. It was the unnatural sounds I was listenin' for, a disturbed bramble or a snapped twig, any little movement what didn't belong. There was nothin'. My stalkers was sittin' as still as dead men.

The moon was gettin' bigger now. Over on my left I heard the soft sounds of a big mountain cat prowlin' on the rocks. A natural sound too. He knew where all of us was. I waited, listenin', goin' slow.

The moon was risin' faster than I wanted it to, lightin' up the mountains and beginnin' to throw shadows from the rocks. It was a Comanche moon all right, big, soft, made for raidin' into Mexico. Quietly I slipped from shadow to shadow, now makin' better time. Another few feet and I would be behind them. Then I could play my first card—the hoot. Then Tied Up could play his card. Then . . . but then I stopped, quick, silent, dead, as still as the rock beside me. There was somethin', a shadow maybe, maybe a rock, a blur in the moonlight. I couldn't tell what it was, but it didn't seem to fit. It was maybe twenty feet away and unmovin'.

But rocks don't breathe and it was breathin'.

I closed my eyes, opened them, closed them again slow and easy and opened them again. Clear and clean I saw him—Missin' Toe. I also saw that he hadn't seen me.

But the trouble was, I couldn't move.

One move, any move, a swallow I think, would've been fatal.

A time or two in my life—I swear it for a fact—I have actually breathed through my eyes. It was the best I could do in competition with those Apaches what can stop their hearts from beatin'. That's what I did now. Quiet and relaxed, I drew fresh clean little puffs of air in through my eyes. Then I slowly breathed out through my nose. I never could figure out why you can breathe in through your eyes but you can't breathe out. If you don't do it too long at a time it also improves the vision, 'specially at night. The important thing was, I wasn't movin' a muscle of my body. I was completely relaxed, limp. One hint of movement on my part, even of breathin', and Missin' Toe would come up shootin'. He always shot first and looked for his target later.

Now I knew my life depended on one thing—patience. I had to stand there totally relaxed until some little flicker of change caused Missin' Toe to turn his head the other way. All I needed was a flicker. I would disappear like I had come, unheard, unseen. Somewhere behind me I heard more rattlesnakes aslither, and over on the rocks the big cat still prowled soft and cautious. The man-smell was botherin' him. I couldn't tell where Poop was, but my Apache mind told me he was on the other side of the rocks from Missin' Toe, coverin' that side of the mountain.

I made a few reckonings on how I might get by them, but I knew I was doin' it more to keep myself calm than for any other reason, 'cause actually my life now depended more on what Missin' Toe did than on anything I could do myself. All I knew for sure was, one move at the wrong time and I was dead—no happy endin' there—though Missin' Toe's shootin' was always in your favor when he was aimin' at you.

And then I saw that I had reckoned without the moon. The moon, like so many things in the heavens during my life, was on my side. As it slowly rose behind me it just as slowly shortened my shadow against the rock that Missin' Toe was lookin' at. In a little while, about the middle of the night, there would be a moment when my shadow would shorten and fade into the earth at the bottom of the rock. That would be the moment I would fade down with it to the ground. The shadow, the rock, the ground would all blend into nothin'.

When I saw that the moon and all the stars in heaven was on my side, I felt a revival of the spirit. I knew I was still a good-luck man and that my life, for all its present danger, was one of those what gets particular attention from the gods. When they truly like somebody they are never stingy with their love.

I watched the shadow shorten. Missin' Toe set there like a rock. I knew he'd not move through the rest of the night. I'd seen Apaches do it for three straight days, sometimes with big red ants crawlin' over them.

Then something unexpected happened, and if I hadn't been a better Apache than Missin' Toe I'da jumped too, like he did, straight up. From in back of me about two arrow flights away there suddenly came the slow mournful wail of what seemed a dyin' wolf, and it was plain to all the wolves and men what could hear it that it wasn't a dyin' wolf or a livin' wolf or any other kind of a wolf. You couldn't much blame Missin' Toe for jumpin'. Tied Up's imitations of animals was about as bad as you could get. But it had come at the right moment and I guessed he had got worried and was beginnin' to play his cards in a different way.

Missin' Toe not only came up, he came up shootin'. And before he'd got the first shot off, which I hoped hit him on his good-toe side, I had faded down the shadows of the trail.

Now all the creatures of night, in the air and on the ground was squawkin' and screamin' and slitherin' at the sound of the pistol shots, which kept goin' on, and about the time I figured Missin' Toe's bullets was runnin' out, I decided to play a card of my own. Instead of givin' the hoot of the owl, I whistled . . . one long low whistle what just meant one thing to one creature on earth. As I started runnin' on down the trail—I would mount him on the run—I heard him comin' through the wild and squawkin' night, his hoofs hammerin' over the rocks with now and then a thunderous bunch of thuds where they hit the grassy spots, and I knew that nothin', absolutely nothin', unless it was a bullet, could stop that horse.

In the distance I heard a volley of shots. That would be Tied Up now, playin' another card. For an instant I fancied I saw him there in his string tie and white shirt and maybe smokin' a little cheroot, cool, calm, unruffled, smilin' and waitin' to see if the odds was good or bad and who was gonna win the deadly game when the hand was finally played. He wouldn't have to wait long. We was playin' the cards fast now. And I was runnin' fast, too, the hammerin' hoofs comin' on behind me, steady, sure, always a little louder. I was runnin' as fast as I could and I don't think Moon Dance even slowed down when he overtook me. His tail was straight out with the wind and I grabbed it, makin' two hops and goin' up on the third, and hearin' as I did so a bullet zing above me in the trees.

Then we was gone, down the trail and into the night, at a tremendous speed. It was tremendous and it was dangerous, but we didn't slow down. We had one more enemy to get by and a few dead men too and my desire in both cases was the same—to get by 'em both as fast as possible.

25

Moon Dance Runs

THAT WAS—there can be no doubt about it—Moon Dance's finest night. From the moment I grabbed his tail and bounced atop him he never faltered. There was rocks and there was gorges and there was canyon rims, but he never shied or slipped or hesitated. He knew—I don't know how—that we was now not only runnin' for our lives but that we was runnin' for home too, Mescalero Town, a hundred miles away. What he didn't know was that he would have to run his heart out to get us there. Or maybe he knew that too. You can never be sure about a horse like that.

We thundered across the grassy knoll beside the treasure without slowin' down, wild creatures of the night risin' up from the trees and scurryin' through the brush. As we neared the gulch, big black buzzards roostin' on the limbs rose up with heavy flaps of their slow-movin' wings. There was hundreds of 'em, black and ugly. From far in back of me I heard more pistol shots and then ahead of me and comin' up fast was Dead Man's Gulch with a dead man in the middle of it. More buzzards rose, so close and thick I had to duck to miss 'em. I was breakin' all the rules now, goin' headlong and blind into a place where no Apache horse likes to go any more than does an Apache himself—where dead men lie. I spoke low words—soft Apache words —to Moon Dance.

And then I caught the stink on the clear night air, strong and ugly, but Moon Dance never slowed. At the gulch—a narrow passage leadin' out onto a slope— he did what I hoped he would do. He rose into the air and sailed high across what must have been Head Toter's remains. After that the air was clean again and the slope fell gently down the mountain towards the desert and the flat cactus lands. That was when I saw a blur over on my right, racin' to cut me off. It was Fantail ridin' wild through the night, too late, I saw, to cut me off, but determined to catch me. He was not only ridin' at breakneck speed along the slope, he was also trailin' a fresh horse with him. Even that wouldn't 've bothered me then, certain as I was of my horse, if two things hadn't happened. First, an arrow whistled by me, close. Second, I remembered that Moon Dance hadn't drunk water now for over two days. In a short race it wouldn't 've mattered. In a long race it might.

So I spoke low words to him again, and down his spine I felt a ripple of understanding. I was holdin' him in till we got out of the mountains. I couldn't afford to waste even an ounce of his energies in useless nervousness.

Another arrow whistled by and I leaned low.

The moon was straight overhead when we turned down the last long slope of Guadalupe Peak and I

could see the desert layin' out before me under the
stars. That was all I asked—the desert flatlands. That
was where Apache horses run their best and where a
horse could prove himself, even a thirsty horse against
two unthirsty ones. Now it was almost straight ahead
for a hundred miles, and I knew every cactus plant and
grain of sand. To myself and to my horse and to the
stars and all the Apache gods, I whispered, "Run,
Moon Dance, run."

It wasn't necessary. Moon Dance knew from the
thud of hoofs behind us that a deadly race was on. He
would run, with or without my urging. You could tell
it from the way he laid his ears back just slightly, gettin'
serious so to speak, and settled down into that long
beautiful stride of his, savin' his strength for the time
when he would need it. There never was an Apache
horse what could resist a race, fair or foul. And there
never was an Apache horse what wasn't smarter than
his master at winnin' one. The trouble was, all three
horses was Apache horses, and both riders Apache
riders.

Moon Dance was runnin' at his best now, easy, fast,
effortless. One horse, any horse, fresh or not, wouldn't
've stood a chance against him, but two fresh horses
was another thing. I let Fantail gain a little, knowin'
he would urge his horse, which would tire him a little.
Then I eased Moon Dance ahead, judgin' by the wind
the exact gait I wanted. I was keepin' just beyond an
arrow's range.

Again I eased Moon Dance and let Fantail again

urge his horse. He took the bait, the teasin' as it's called. I could hear his horse's hoofs poundin' a little faster, a little closer. He was urgin' him hard. What I was doin' easy and without effort to my horse was causin' Fantail to grow nervous, thinkin' he was gainin', and push his horse too hard. It's the surest way in the world to tire a horse, not only for the extra effort but the extra wear and tear on his nervous system. Horses when they run, really run, don't like to be kicked around. Easily then, with no effort, so slowly the night wind scarcely changed in my face, I let Moon Dance pick up again. He knew the game as well as I did, maybe better, and maybe Fantail knew it too, but Fantail was behind and tryin' to catch up and that made all the difference. Each time I teased him in this manner I could hear his horse fall behind a step or two. Slowly, very slowly, Moon Dance was wearin' the other horse out.

And then I heard what I had known I would hear— the last hard burst of speed from the worn horse. Fantail was ridin' him to his death, gettin' the last final effort out of him before changin' to the fresh horse. I could hear him comin' on, givin' everything he had. When he was at his limit, Fantail changed horses. He did a good job of changin', never broke stride. It ain't easy. And now I knew he'd push the fresh horse as hard as he could be pushed. He would urge him and urge him, in a desperate attempt to catch up.

I was right. The thuds, now of a single horse, was comin' closer. He was gainin'. Not only was he a fresh

horse, he was a good horse. If Moon Dance was bothered by the oncomin' hoofbeats, he gave no sign of it.
He kept his stride and I didn't argue with him or urge
him or try to play the teasin' game any more. How
tired he was, I didn't know. How long he could keep
up that terrible pace, I didn't know either. But he
knew. So from that moment on, as far as I was concerned, it was horse against horse. When you're in
doubt or when you're in trouble, leave it to the horse.
I leaned low over his neck, makin' myself a part of
him.

Everything now was a wild blur of stars and cactus
flyin' by. And the wind, always the wind, seemin' to
caress Moon Dance's flyin' mane. I knew his long black
tail was straight out, streamin'. Beneath me I could
feel the smooth and even power of his tremendous
stride. He hadn't once changed his pace since I turned
the runnin' over to him.

Fantail was urgin' hard now, gainin' fast. It was the
only chance he had. He knew it and I knew it. He had
to close while that horse was fresh. And he was closin',
fast. The hoofbeats grew steadily closer, louder,
seemin' to be somewhere not far behind Moon Dance's
streamin' tail. Still Moon Dance kept his pace. It was
as if he was now playin' a teasin' game of his own, except he was playin' it slower and more dangerous than
the one I'd played before, lettin' the horse come on,
always a little closer. And I guess he knew what he was
doin', 'cause after he had done this for what seemed a
dangerously long time and I was beginnin' to wonder if

he was beginnin' to tire and the other horse was almost upon us, he laid his ears back just a little more and put on the most beautiful slow burst of speed I have ever felt beneath me from a horse. It was as if he had reservoirs of energy, as if maybe he might even, if he so wished, humiliate the other horse by pullin' clear out of sight. But he didn't. He pulled ahead a ways, easy and sure, almost out of arrow range, and then eased back into that long beautiful stride, his ears raisin' back up to where they had been before. It took my breath away, so easily had he done it.

And it must've done somethin' to Fantail too, scared him, maybe demoralized him, 'cause it was then that he did what not only led to his defeat in that wild race beneath the stars but what also marked him forever as the stupidest of men—horseracin' men, that is—worthy in the future only of my contempt.

Seein' us pull away so easy, and just when he had been so close, he lost the one thing you can't ever lose and win . . . his control. He did what only a desperate, which is to say a losin', man would do. He went wild, berserk, crazy, and started shootin' arrows. It wasn't that he was shootin' at my back what brought my contempt—that was fair play for Fantail—but that he was throwin' his horse off stride and tirin' him with every arrow he shot. In such a race as that, between two such horses, even the smallest movement against the horse's stride can ruin everything. It not only tires the horse, it confuses him. Good riders become part of the horse. I myself had never once turned around to look behind me, knowin' it would be a wasteful burden, tiny but still wasteful, for Moon Dance, and knowin' too that his respect for my intelligence would suffer. You can't do that and expect your horse to run his best. But Fantail was now shootin' arrows at the moon and all the stars in a kind of childish frenzy, and I knew then that Moon Dance and I would win the race. My only thought was that we deserved a better enemy.

Despite Fantail's stupidness, the horse put up a good fight, for a while. But it was too much to ask of any horse. After a time, when Moon Dance was latherin' good and beginnin' to breathe a little hard himself, I heard the pursuin' thuds fade slowly away behind me into the night. No horse—especially no Apache horse —would run his heart out for a stupid master. Back there somewhere the horse had limped to a tremblin' halt in the sand and cactus plants, like a horse will do when he's worn completely out and his spirit of winnin' is dead.

I patted Moon Dance's latherin' neck, slowed him gradually to a gentle lope, held him there for a while, then eased him to a walk. He was still prancin' and snortin'—good horses is hard to stop—his head still tossin', froth flyin' through the air. And when I patted him a second time he gave a gentle whinny and flung up his tail in, I think, horsely disrespect for the man and beast back there, and maybe for all the men and beasts on earth who think they can catch an Apache horse what loves his master.

26

Goodbye Goodbye

THERE'S BEEN TIMES in my life when I wished I was a
Navajo, so I could raise my voice to all the desert stars
and sing to them of travelin' in beauty. That was now
the way I felt as I crossed the desert floor beneath a
dyin' moon and seen the distant mountains of my
home. I was at peace with everything, and so was my
horse. The last stars was fadin' and the desert was
turnin' from color to color and the world was clean,
pure, quiet. There was no way for me to tell that world
so morning-sweet just how I felt, except to sing, and
the only song what seemed to fit was the Navajo
chant.

But I was now a pure Apache.

The sun had not yet risen when Moon Dance and
I turned up Dog Canyon toward Mescalero Town.
This was goin' to be another good-luck day—good for
livin', fightin', dyin'. Every bird and bush and rock
and creature was in its right and fittin' place. And it
was right and fittin' that I do what I did then. Only
on such a mornin' could I have done it in the way I felt
was true and proper.

Apaches don't usually say goodbye, either to each

other or their horses, most especially not to their horses. But I had by now broke all the rules; to break another one would make no difference. Curlin' down Dog Canyon I took a familiar trail to the pastures of Cuts Plenty Throats, and after a few soft words of horse talk which I ain't gonna tell, I told Moon Dance goodbye and let him know that he was free to join the herd again.

He galloped away, horse-happy with the mornin', snortin' and frolickin'. And then he did what I hoped he'd do—turned around after a little canter and came back, whinnyin' and nose-nudgin' me in the backside. That was his way of tellin' me that a loyal horse never says goodbye, that he'd always be there when I needed him.

I left him there then, standin' on the hill in the wind, and moved up the mountain trail to the wickiups around the town, notin' that though all the birds was singin' and the campfires was burnin' and a few old women was doin' laundry and the kids was dirty with play, the dogs wasn't barkin'. That could only mean one thing.

But how had he known, Old Wickiup, that I had found the gold? How had he known that on this good-luck day I would return? Someone, I guessed, had sent a signal. However he had known it, one thing was certain. The dogs wasn't barkin'. Mescalero Town lay quiet in the sun. And the quietness seemed to say that the chief was expectin' me.

I found him at his wickiup, makin' his preparations.

Mad Woman, as usual, was drapin' clothes over a greasewood bush and mumblin' words too low to hear. The chief paid no attention to her.

He seemed completely unsurprised to see me, but I had learned long ago that nothing, absolutely nothing, could surprise him.

"Welcome, my son," he said.

"Grandfather," I said. "I know."

"Good, my son. That is very good."

"Grandfather," I said. "I know who I am."

"That is good, my son."

"Grandfather," I said. "I know other things."

"Today I go on a journey, my son."

"Grandfather," I said. "I know everything."

"Do not brag, my son. Not on a day like this. Hand me my lance."

"I want you to know," I said, "that I know."

"Hand me my feathers."

"May I ask a question, Grandfather?"

"Hand me my blanket."

"I am the only one who knows, Grandfather."

"Hand me my rattle."

He had his baggage now, a clutterance of his life, and was half draggin' it down the trail. After a few steps, he turned, the feathers droopin' from one hand, his lance from the other, a crazy old hat on his head. "You say you know?"

"Yes, Grandfather."

Very softly then he said, "But you will never tell, my son."

And to this day I've never known for sure exactly how he meant it.

He started off again, and again turned back.

"What was your question, my son?"

"Why, Grandfather, why?"

"The gods move in mysterious ways."

"No. Why did you send them?"

I think he smiled, a flicker, a kind of smile that seemed to say he was much pleased with himself.

"You are forgetting something, my son. I sent Missing Toe."

So he had known all that too, even before it happened. I *was* forgetting something—the most important thing—and I was sorry I had asked.

Missin' Toe don't count. The words came back to me. Now they made perfect Apache sense.

He was draggin' his baggage off down the trail then and I was standin' there in the silence, Mad Woman keenin' low. In a little while I heard his song begin in the canyon below. It was low and long, a quiet song on a good-luck day, risin' slowly to the sky, perfectly in tone with the earth on which I knew he was squatted.

As later I made my way to the shack where I lived, I saw a dreary little procession comin' up the trail from the desert floor. Two boys—Poop and Fantail—was ridin' one horse and leadin' another over which was hangin' a body. It wasn't a dead body but a live body, and word was already circulatin' around the town that Missin' Toe—by God—had shot off his other toe.

27

In the Aftertime

THERE'S TWO THINGS I'll never do, unless I have to—lie or brag. The first is sinful and the second brings bad luck. What I have told you is the truth, and what I have yet to tell you is also the truth.

First I must tell you that nothin' much has changed in this part of the world since the time of my adventure, just as nothin' much had changed in all the moons before it. If Coronado came ridin' up the trail tomorrow, he would find us, the Mescaleros, much the same. The mountains is still the same and so is the desert. The moon still shines on Mescalero Town and on that place in the Guadalupes where rests the Apache gold and the bones of them what wanted it. Sometimes when the moon is big I take some of the young chiefs with me and ride across the cactus lands to the mountains and up Dead Man's Gulch past the treasure to the rim of the earth at Suicide Leap. I never tell them why I do that, and they, bein' good Apaches, never ask. Nor do I tell them why we have a horse race under the stars across the desert on the way back. When by chance the talk turns to tales about the legend and the gold, I always put on my wisest expression and say, "Be patient, my sons, be patient." And when the talk turns to horses, I say nothin'.

I must also tell you that Tied Up comes to see me now and then. He is always cool and clean no matter what the temperature, and usually someone has stolen his horse or robbed him on the way. By the way, he never did locate the gold. He tells me the mountains is infested again with varmints of the kind we met before, all lookin' for but none findin' the treasure—shootin' at each other mostly. Of course I knew that, it bein' part of my duty to see that the gold is kept a secret.

I dislike mentionin' unimportant things, but you may be curious so I will tell you. Missin' Toe got well. He now limps a little on both feet. I ordered that his gun be taken from him and given to the children to play with, they bein' more reliable and safe and better shots too, prob'ly. Nor did I, after my elevation in the tribe, punish Poop and Fantail, though I must confess that for many moons I made them do women's work and disallowed either of them to carry a knife or go near a horse. There's some things that even an Apache can't cancel from his memory.

And finally I must tell you this. I hope the tale that I have told is to your liking, no matter what your tribe or clan or color, and I hope the story of the treasure helps to keep your wonderment alive through all your moons, but most of all I hope that nowhere in my tale of the Apaches and their gold have I written words unworthy of one who bears the honored name of Chief Good Luck Arizona Man.